Advance Praise

"I enjoyed reading this fun and unique approach to learning a new language. Andrew Pham offers an easy guide to understanding the formation of language families and their benefit. This book will help many of us learn a new language quickly and effectively than conventional methods.
--Maria Legros, MA Student, Kingston University, London, UK

This is a terrific book in that it not only provides us with how-to advice but also with examples of what the author had developed for himself to learn to become a polyglot during all these years. I found what Andrew Pham said about overlearning so true that I have gone back to my own learning approach and revised it accordingly. A really great book.
--Rebecca Thoreau, Soccer Mom, Texas

"The narrative and conversational style bring the language learners to the study with fresh glee and a uniquely applicable approach. I strongly recommend it to both the poly- and uni-glots."
--Silas K. Grossberndt, Columbia University, Senior

"This book is not only easy read but also very easy to understand. I find this book's sections on the fundamentals of Chinese grammar, verb and vocabulary to be particularly well written, concise and to the point. What I find the most remarkable about this book is that it not only deals with how we should learn, but also what to learn, when and why.

Funny and progressive, this book ends with a roadmap for us to follow – and a reminder of what not to do in learning languages. Remarkable."
--Steven Li, Trilingual, Queens, New York

How to Speak Any Language in 1 Month & Never Forget It

A Polyglot's Journey Into the Wonderland of Language Learning

Andrew Pham
CEO
Accelerated Proactive Learning, Inc.

About the author:

At 21 years old, Andrew Pham was a young Vietnamese student living in Paris. Even though he did not call himself a polyglot, he already spoke five languages at the time: French, Spanish, Portuguese, German, and his native Vietnamese.

Fast forward to the present time, he currently speaks nine languages among a dozen he knows—but the difference is that, now, it only takes him about 1 month, rather than several months or years, to learn each new language.

A senior member of the Institute of Electronics and Electrical Engineering (IEEE), Andrew Pham is also the creator of AnyLanguagein1Month.com platform and the CEO of Accelerated Proactive Learning, Inc.

Prior to this book, Andrew Pham's most recent book was From Business Strategy to Information Technology Roadmap. A Practical Guide for Executives and Board Members, published by CRC Press (an imprint of Francis & Taylor Group), 2013.

Copyright © 2017, Andrew Pham. All right reserved.

Published by Accelerated Proactive Learning, Inc.

"Any Language in 1 Month" is a registered trademark owned by Accelerated Proactive Learning, Inc.

This book or any portion thereof may not be reproduced, stored, transmitted by any means, or used in any manner whatsoever without the express written permission of the copyright holder, except for the use of brief quotations in a book review.

Disclaimer:

The author and publisher have tried to provide accurate information in this book. However, the author and publisher present the information only "as is", without any warranty of accuracy or completeness, and can't be held responsible for any errors, omissions or contrary interpretations of the subject matter herein. There shall be no liability to any person or entity for loss or damage to be caused, directly or indirectly, by information contained within this book.

This book is published for motivational and informational purposes only.

We would appreciate it if readers would call our attention to any errors or outdated information at: contact@acceleratedproactivelearning.com

Print ISBN: 978-0999279199
EBook ISBN: 978-0999279144

Table of Contents

Chapter 1: Introduction 9

Chapter 2: Why do people want to learn a foreign language? 11

Chapter 3: Why do some people succeed while others fail to learn a new foreign language? 14

Chapter 4: Why did I want to learn foreign languages? 19

Chapter 5: From not properly speaking French to mastering it…to speaking Spanish, Portuguese, and German without pain 22

Chapter 6: What did I do to "unload" my extreme knowledge of French parts of speech and syntax? 33

Chapter 7: What did I do to "lower" my knowledge of French verb tenses to speak as a regular person? ... 42

Chapter 8: What did I do with Spanish parts of speech and syntax when I first started to learn it? 52

Chapter 9: What else did I do to my list of Spanish verb tenses before I took the first flight to Spain? 63

Chapter 10: What are the two things I also did that helped me be comfortable speaking Spanish for such a long time thereafter? 79

Chapter 11: Which foreign languages of what family of languages should you learn to speak first? 86

Chapter 12: How to build up your Russian, Arabic, Swahili, Chinese, and Japanese vocabulary fast? 99

Chapter 13: What did I do to learn to speak Italian in three and a half weeks? 112

Chapter 14: How did I learn to speak Mandarin Chinese in four weeks? 131

Chapter 15: How did I recover my Portuguese in two weeks for the Olympics Games in Rio? 152

Chapter 16: All the things you should not do in learning to speak a foreign language in a nutshell 189

Chapter 17: How not to forget a foreign language you have learned? 192

Chapter 18: Epilogue 196

Chapter 1: Introduction

Without intentionally working hard to become one, I have been fortunate enough over the years to be one of those polyglots, meaning someone who speaks several languages, that people admire. If you're reading this book, I would guess that it is not only because you generally admire polyglots but also, if not mainly, because you're intrigued by the book title and would like to know how to effectively learn a foreign language in one month and never forget it. If that is what you're looking for, you have come to the right place.

But before I share with you how I learned, I will first walk you through some of the reasons why people want to learn a foreign language, and why, while some succeed, many fail. I will also share with you my own reasons for learning foreign languages and how I came to succeed: What did I do that others did not?

Rather than providing you with just a compilation of high-level "how-to" suggestions, I will share with you examples of grammar and verb summaries I developed for myself while I was learning French, Spanish, Italian, Portuguese, and even Chinese. Furthermore, I will also share with you how to quickly build up your new vocabulary in Russian, Arabic, Swahili, Chinese, and Japanese. This way, you can either learn directly from what I created for myself or be inspired to create your own. In other words, I will share with you not only how I successfully learned all the languages I learned but also what portions of grammar and verb tenses I learned, when, and why.

Chapter 2: Why do people want to learn a foreign language?

While many people try to learn a foreign language, most often fail to say anything beyond a few words, much less sustain a conversation. While some of you may not see the connection at first, I know, from experience, that examining the reasons why people want to learn a foreign language will help us understand, along with some other reasons, why some succeed while many fail.

First, there are the students in schools or colleges who must learn a foreign language as part of their curriculum. For this group of learners, the reason for learning a language is mainly to pass an exam and to have good grades in school. This is to say that there is not too much personal excitement in languages here. In addition, while these students learn, their focus is essentially on writing and reading rather than on speaking. Although the distinction between learning to speak and learning to read and write may seem innocent, learning to speak, read and write often requires so much time that many adult learners end up being sucked away by other life responsibilities in the meantime—letting their learning slip or fall completely to the wayside.

Beyond this, there is also a large difference between knowing how to read a language, how to write it, and how to speak it. I know this well since this is what happened to me when I was still a young man in high school. At the time, I was considered by my high school teachers and friends to be a very good student in French—supposedly in all aspects of the French language. It was not until I landed in Paris, many years ago, that I came to realize that I could barely say a few sentences in real-life situations in French to some people with whom I was speaking. More on this later.

Let's now return to our different categories of language learners. Aside from the students above, more people want, nowadays, to learn a foreign language because they think they can use it to either get a promotion or a transfer to another country for international experience. This had led, in the past, to the increase in popularity of the Japanese language, then during the last ten or fifteen years of Chinese, and more recently of Vietnamese.

In addition to the two groups of learners above, there are also many other people who want to learn a foreign language because they either like the country or like the people from that country. While this certainly sounds great, many of these people unfortunately often end up not being able to speak or engage in any serious conversations with anyone in the new language. This time, however, the reason is not because they are not interested in languages, but mainly because the approach they take to learn the new language, may not be a very good one. To illustrate this, imagine the way some people often skip several days of learning and only come back to spend several hours in one or two days in a row to catch up on all the lessons they missed, thinking that if they accomplish the same number of lessons by a given point in time, they should be fine. We will examine, in more depth, the reasons why many people fail to effectively learn a new language in the next chapter, but I know that skipping days—or learning only once a week—is not the best way to learn a new language. Besides the fact that this often breaks the momentum, it also leads people to forget what they have previously learned, making it difficult to effectively build up the next layer of knowledge.

Chapter 3: Why do some people succeed while others fail to learn a new foreign language?

From the previous chapter, you can guess that most people approach the language learning process rather passively. This means that they often do not have too much personal interest in being able to speak, read or write a new language before a certain timeframe. Except, maybe, for the students who need to take their exams by a certain date. In other words, most of these people don't have the sense of urgency needed to create a plan and/or a proper timeline to follow. While having a plan and a short timeframe within which to work might sound constraining, it is, in fact, one of the best contributing factors to people succeeding in learning a language.

Now, if you're not already convinced that many people learn languages without a specific timeline, just look around you. You will be surprised to discover how many people you know, maybe even yourself, don't have an idea as to when they should be able to speak, read or write in the new language. Very often, it is "Que sera sera!" ("Whatever will be will be!"). Exception made for very young learners with little or no responsibility in life, you will understand why many of these people often end up quitting during the process, essentially due to all the things they must do to take care of their adult life or their family's life. In the end, it is not uncommon to hear people say, "Sorry. I did five years of Spanish but can only say a few words!" or "I learned French for two years in college but only remember a few sentences", and so forth and so on.

Besides this lack of plan or timeline, the second reason why many people fail to learn a foreign language is the lack of concentration, often encouraged by this type of refrain: "Just drive to work while listening to our recordings, and you will speak Spanish in no time!" Amongst all the other prevalent myths in language learning, this should be ranked among one of the top reasons why people fail, if not the top reason.

A third often cited reason why many people fail is because they aim very early on to learn to speak like a native, with a "true French accent"! Now, don't get me wrong. I'm not saying that you should avoid having a perfect "native" accent. But the main goal of speaking a foreign language, for me, should be, first and foremost, to understand what people are saying and be understood by the very people with whom you are speaking in that language. Whether you speak with a perfect "native" accent or not is only secondary, regardless of whether it is at the beginning, middle, or end of your learning.

To show you why speaking a foreign language with a true native accent is not important, just remember that one of the U.S. Supreme Court Justices is none other than Justice Sonia Sotomayor. As everyone who has heard her speak would agree, it is obvious that she speaks English with a rather Spanish-like accent. The same is true of Henry Kissinger, former Secretary of State, who is known to speak English with a rather heavy German-leaning accent. In either case, they both speak heavily accented English— but, at the same time, are considered by many of us to have achieved more than what most Americans with a perfect accent could hope to achieve.

The fourth reason why I think many people end up not being able to speak the language they learn, is because they tend to spend time reading more on culture rather than acquiring the new language first.

At the same time, many learners mistakenly think that if they can hear all the explanations in the base language, that will allow them to continue to run on the treadmill or drive to work without having to even focus on their lesson. It is as if these learners believe that all the sudden some sort of miracle will happen to enable them to naturally speak the new language. For having successfully learned all the languages I have learned, I know that this has never worked and will never work. At best, it is only a dream, and, at worst, an illusion.

On the other hand, some learners believe that if they could learn as they believe children do—by listening and by repeating words they see in some images along with some aural explanations in the target language—, then they should be able to speak soon and as well as they believe children do. While this sounds interesting, it may be more effective for young children (who have plenty of time and practically no worries about life), rather than for the adult learners (who are often too busy and who have plenty of worries) to be able to follow such method for a long time without interruption. As surprisingly strange as it might sound, some other adult learners even believe that the only thing they would only need to do, as they also believe children do, is to listen and repeat sentences, while not having to worry about learning grammar. I don't know if I could ever say this more clearly than this, but learning to speak a foreign language without learning grammar will never make you a solid speaker. It is like when someone wants to learn to play drums, but does not learn to read music notation. While he or she can play somewhat alone, but it will be impossible for him or her to play in harmony with other musicians. In the case of language learning, this would mean that whenever someone wants to learn a new language without learning grammar, he or she might be able to say a few words or, at best, some sentences, but conversing with others on their own would be impossible—unless they have many months or years to spend on language learning. In both the above two cases, believing that we can just get the adult learners to mimic the way children we believe how children learn without any modifications is to believe that psychologically adult learners and young children have the same need and behave the same way. Unfortunately, neither is true.

Besides all the reasons above, there is also the fact that when learning a new foreign language, many people mistakenly think that the thicker the books or the more downloads they get, the better it will be. Besides the mistaken feeling that they are getting a lot of content's worth for their money, this often leads them to be overwhelmed by the volume of material they receive. Sometimes, it is such that the learners get lost after a few weeks and start letting their focus slide. Now, do not get me wrong. If your intent is to become an intellectual or a professional writer in a foreign language with three or four years to spare, then it could be different. But if you want to be able to converse with people about daily life topics in a new language in some foreseeable future, then you should learn differently—a little bit at a time. Like many things in life, before you can run, you must learn to crawl and walk first. It is as if "less is more."

Finally, I have seen some people who want to speak a foreign language, but because they want to speak with a perfect grammar or because they are so shy that they end up never saying anything or asking any question. Along with some other rule I have already shared with you above, another rule you should remember when learning a new language is to be curious and to like to practice not only speaking in general but also conversing, meaning taking part in a rather meaningful conversation, from day one—or, as I would say, from the first few minutes.

Chapter 4: Why did I want to learn foreign languages?

For many people, learning a new language is like a chore; for people like myself, it is a different story. Since I was very young, I was already interested in knowing more about other countries and cultures. To this effect, I was very interested in interacting with people in their own language. Intuitively, I thought that that would make me more well-rounded and people would like me much more if I could speak with them in their language—and they did.

Without following any order of importance, below are the main reasons why I have wanted to learn foreign languages:

1.   Seeing a new perspective:

Rather than liking people who would agree with me about everything, I was, even when I was much younger, interested in hearing different perspectives than mine or engaging with someone who disagreed with me. What I mean to say is that, rather than being bothered by the fact that someone might have a different opinion from me, I was attracted to it—to know why someone, because of his or her culture, would have such a different perspective other than mine. This is very much like the way the late Flora Lewis used to say: "Learning another language is not learning different words for the same thing, but learning another way to think about things."

2. Discovering a new culture:

It is not to say that I'm a man of world culture, but I have always liked to know about other people's cultures—and, to some degree, even more now than when I was much younger. The way I look at foreign languages, I see them as a helping hand or bridges into these cultures. (This said, I never spend time reading about culture during my language lessons.)

3. Making new friends:

I hope this will not come as a big revelation to anyone, but when I was young, I liked to have a lot of friends. Years later, after I got married and started to have children of my own, things became different. With the responsibility of being a parent, time became scarce, and with the hard work we had to put into raising our kids, the desire, time, and energy it took to meet with new friends also became scarcer. But everything was different when I was much younger and before the children arrived.

4. Learning a new way of cooking and eating:

I have always liked to eat different kinds of food, even more now than ever before. This is the reason why I'm glad to say that I have tasted food from all the countries or territories I have visited throughout the years, not only from France, Spain, Belgium, England, Andorra, Holland, Austria, Switzerland, Germany, Sweden, Denmark, Israel, and the UAE, but also from Puerto Rico, Norway, Italy, and more recently, Japan and Iceland.

5. Acquiring a new "life" (and, along with that, a completely new knowledge):

With everything I have mentioned above, I see language learning as a good way to acquire another life in that culture—and completely new knowledge along with it. This is to say that while one does not need to be intelligent to succeed at learning a new language, it generally makes us smarter with every new language we know.

With all the above reasons, you can be sure that I saw, and still see, foreign language learning, not as a hassle or something I must do, but as a joy and something exciting to go through.

Chapter 5: From not properly speaking French to mastering it…to speaking Spanish, Portuguese, and German without pain

Among the first foreign languages I learned was French and German. Even though I was considered a very good student in French in high school, I was not actually very good at speaking French in real-life situations. Even so, most of what I could say or the way I said it was like the way royals talked in the early 20th century. In other words, the way I talked, while somewhat charming for some people I interacted with, made me sound like someone who came directly out of Victor Hugo's masterpiece.

To give you a few examples of the way I used to speak at the time, below are some of the sentences I still remember I used to say: "Seriez-vous aimable d'annoncer à madame que je suis arrivé?" ("Would you please announce to milady that I have arrived?"), or "C'est un grand honneur de vous recontrer" ("It is a great honor to meet you"), or still, "Permettez-moi, s'il vous plaît, de me retirer" ("Please, allow me to withdraw"), etc.

Apart from a mildly charming side to this manner of speaking, it was clearly strange. For this reason, I quickly decided that I should quickly improve my speaking ability and "lower" my French standard by making it less formal.
Once I made my decision, I studied every day, reading and circling new words that I thought would be useful for me to speak with people and looking them up in the dictionary. To enhance my listening skills, I sometimes went to the

Georges Pompidou Centre in the evening to listen to some of their language recordings, even borrowing them to listen to overnight. Another thing I found myself doing was speaking to myself when no friends of mine were around to help me practice speaking.

In parallel to the above, I also started a quick review of all the French parts of speech and verb tenses to try to figure out why people considered my French to be so "upper class." I will share more with you, in the next two chapters, what I specifically did to "unclutter" my French before I could become better at speaking. But, let's say, for now, that thanks to my focus, my French improved quickly thereafter—and so much so that I went on, a few years later, to obtain a few degrees from some well-known French universities. From this experience with French, I retained the idea that to be effective at learning a new foreign language, we should always learn with focus and I would even say with passion.

The next foreign language I learned was Spanish. While living in Paris, I met with many Latino students either at the university or during my meals at the beautiful Cité Internationale Universitaire in the outskirts of Paris. Many of them were Argentinians, Peruvians, and Mexicans. As everyone can relate to, people from Latin America are known to be open and friendly. For this reason, I quickly made a lot of Latino friends—practically in no time. While they all spoke French, I started to be intrigued by their Spanish in which they sometimes inevitably spoke with one another while we were meeting up.

Curious, I went home and started to learn a few Spanish words. A week or two after, when our group of friends met again, I surprised everyone by saying a few words in Spanish. At first, some of them thought that I only wanted to make some jokes, but as I continued, many of them started to interrupt their own conversations to listen to what I was saying. The reason why they took notice was not because I said something fancy, but more because they suddenly realized that I had made some personal effort to learn their mother tongue. After realizing this, some of them started to stop talking between themselves to help me, either by correcting my pronunciation or by teaching me one or two more new words to help me expand my vocabulary. It was then that I realized how much Nelson Mandela was right when he said that: "If you speak with a man in a language he understands, that goes to his head. If you speak to a man in his mother tongue, that goes to his heart."

With the helping hand of some of my Latino friends, I soon started to make more solid progress in Spanish, something that has given me, ever since, plenty of opportunities to have fun interacting with people. It has even helped me get served an extra amount of food whenever I would drop by our local deli, especially in Texas (where we lived for several years), during which I would speak in Spanish to some of the Latinos who worked there. First, they looked almost startled. But after I said in Spanish, somewhat jokingly, that I, too, came from a Latin American country, they started invariably to smile and responded back to me in their native Spanish— and almost always, with an extra serving of meat or vegetables. Besides this nice little benefit, I also discovered, sometime later, that knowing Spanish also enabled me to easily read and understand Catalan during a trip my wife and I made to Andorra. A beautiful sovereign principality, Andorra is located between the Southeast of France and Spain in a region which many locals from the Spanish side refer to as Catalonia.

From the experience I had with Spanish, I retained the fact that, in language learning, we should not hesitate to speak even if that means making some mistakes. Rather than being ashamed of our mistakes, we should be happy that people are understanding most of what we are saying while also helping us to become better speakers by pointing out whatever mistakes we might be making. This is to say that we should not become upset when someone offers to correct us, but instead, thank them for their help. After all, we would rather be corrected when we first start learning a foreign language than speak incorrectly for the next twenty years, only to realize later that our French or Spanish had never been completely correct.

I will share with you in more detail what I did to become so good in Spanish in a few more chapters, but let's say, for now, that I became very fluent a year or two after I started to learn Spanish.

While it was not part of a plan, as soon as I became fluent in Spanish, I started to become interested in Portuguese. The reasons for my interest came essentially from the many people from Portugal I bumped into, at work and around my neighborhood. Given the fact that I had already had some solid knowledge of French and Spanish at the time, learning Portuguese proved to be quite straightforward for me. While it is tempting to attribute the successful result of my learning Portuguese to my intellect alone, the main reason, I believe, is because it falls within the same family of Italic or Romance languages as French and, especially, Spanish.

Some of you might be wondering how I could be sure that the main reason I was able to learn Portuguese was because it is of the same family of languages as French and Spanish. Why am I this sure? The reason is because one day while walking along the Seine river on the other side of the Notre Dame cathedral, I came across a small book entitled "Gramática Concisa Espanhola" ("Concise Spanish Grammar") entirely in Portuguese, but which teaches Spanish. Curious, I opened it and got so captivated that I bought it a few minutes later and went straight home to read it until late into the night. The more I read, the more I had the feeling that Portuguese had been invented by the same people who had invented Spanish. The book was so well written and so clear in its explanation of Spanish grammar and verbs, I went back to it again the next day and again the day after until everything became clear in my mind. From what I remember even until today, I read it a total of five or six times during that week until I had the impression, a few days later, that I had already known Portuguese.

To be clear, this was not really my first encounter with the so-called family of languages. Having learned Spanish after French, I had coincidentally come across some words in

Spanish that were like their French counterparts, but that was it. What strikes me the most here is that what I was reading in that Portuguese book was so close to Spanish that I had the feeling that the book was written in Spanish—rather than in Portuguese. The second thing that got me so excited with the book was that while I was not learning Spanish at the time (because I had already become good at it), the fact that I could guess or understand practically everything I was reading in Portuguese was such that it dramatically increased my belief that successfully learning Portuguese would be easy for me. Even until this day, you would not be surprised to know that I still read books on grammar or verbs of a language I had already learned in the new language that I'm trying to learn. Sometimes, I would switch around by reading books in a language I had already learned to learn the new language. This is, for example, something I did with German books which I bought from Amazon Germany (Amazon.de) to read on Russian grammar.

While I enjoyed living in Paris and speaking Portuguese with some of the people I knew from my neighborhood, due to some personal reasons, I had to move away from where I was living at the time. As a result, I lost the opportunity to practice Portuguese with some of the nicest Portuguese people I had ever met. Remember that this was before the arrival of Facebook, Instagram, Twitter, Snapchat, etc., and when there was no iPhone to keep in touch with one another like today. Being unable to continue practicing speaking Portuguese, which I really like for its exotic sound, is something I regretted for a long time thereafter—until one day when I had the opportunity to quickly "recover" it in time to attend the Olympics Games in Rio. More on this later.

A few years into my living in Paris, I decided to pursue German or, to be more exact, to continue German, which I had already learned at the Goethe Institute in Saigon when I was a high school student in Vietnam. Hearing this, I guess some of you might think that I'm a geek with languages—an exception of sorts. If that is what you think, then you will be wrong because the reality was only that I had thought, towards the end of my high school years, that I might want to learn German to get ready to apply to go to Germany whereby I could pursue a higher education in Engineering.

But rather than going to Germany this time around, I decided to take this opportunity to go to Austria, and more precisely to Vienna, the capital of Austria. Too much time has passed since then for me to remember exactly how Vienna was at the time, but from my memory, it was a very clean and beautiful city—with everyone, or almost everyone, knowing how to play a classical instrument. Music was, so to speak, in the air, and free concerts were almost everywhere. I was young, innocent, and excited to discover a new country and a beautiful city.

A few days after I got settled down, I went to Wiener Universität where I enrolled into a Mittelstufe (mid-level) German class, a course which, at the time, was rather advanced in that it was somewhat, from what I remember, geared towards foreign students who would aim to pursue their higher education in a German-speaking university.

Many years have gone by, and I don't remember exactly now how I got into that rather advanced class level, whether it was because I took a test or because of my previous German certificate from the Goethe Institute. But being so young, I was very proud of myself. It was only after the first few weeks after the class had begun that I realized that I might have made a "mistake" by enrolling in a course at that rather advanced level. To avoid keeping you in suspense for too long, let's just say that while I did well in my German class, I came to realize that there were grammar concepts I had missed from previous levels, making it a bit difficult for me to be among the best in the class. Not a day went by without me realizing that while I did fine in the class, I somewhat had an issue with some of the reading and writing exercises. From this experience with German, I realized that it is difficult to learn to effectively speak, read, and write a new language at the same time, especially in hoping to achieve everything in a few short months.

This said, being young at the time and eager to show how smart I was, I went on studying with a lot of intensity, successfully graduating from the class without pain. Vienna was beautiful; I was happy and proud of myself.

With the knowledge gained from my days at Wiener Universität, I caught my wife's relatives by surprise by speaking in German with their German friends from Tübingen when my wife and I drove to visit them in Germany. Another benefit I gained from my knowledge of German was that it also enabled me, along with my knowledge of English, to easily read Dutch when my wife and I had the opportunity to visit beautiful Holland for the magnificent tulips. On top of this, knowing German now also enables me to catch up with what is going on around the world with a European perspective whenever I would get online to read the news on FAZ (Frankfurter Allgemeine Zeitung) or on the Deutsche Welle (DW). Otherwise, regularly reading the news or listening to German radio is also something I must do to maintain my knowledge of German.

With all my successes at language learning, you might wonder if there is anything other than a class or some helping hands from friends that I had that helped me so easily learn all these foreign languages?

Without the following being in any specific order of importance, below are some of the other things I did, which did help me a lot:

1.   Speak from day one:

Even now, one of the mistakes people often commit is thinking that they should only speak after they know all the grammar or verb tenses. Desiring to be perfect may not be a problem by itself, but wanting to know perfect grammar before you can even say a sentence or two is something that hurts rather than helps you speak the new language. From what I have gone through in terms of learning, especially after learning all the languages I have learned, I can assure you that you should not worry about your grammar or accent too much, at least at the beginning. To the contrary, you should not hesitate to speak aloud and as soon and as often as you can, even if you know that not everything you say will be grammatically perfect. Likewise, if you ever catch yourself translating what you say in the target language from your base language, that should be fine, at least during the first weeks. As you know, Rome was not built in a day, so feel free to give yourself some slack to get used to speaking in the new language first. One day, you will be delighted to realize suddenly that you are no longer translating from the base language into the target language—as I had observed in my own situation.

2. Listen to the radio:

While people on the radio do tend to speak fast, especially when we are not as good at understanding at first, their speed may appear even faster than it is. But just like anything else, do not give up. One day you will be surprised to see that you will start understanding more;

3. Watch TV with subtitles in the new language (yes, with sub-titles in the new target language):

This is something I enjoy doing a lot, even if I know that it is often recommended that you watch TV without subtitles in the target language. This may be something you can do when you are at an advanced stage, but early on, feel free to watch TV and look at the subtitles in that new language at the same time. This is what I did very often many years ago—and which I still do even until now, together with my wife.

4. Study as regularly as possible:

More now than ever before, whenever I learn a new language, I always study regularly—at least, one or two days a week back then and, more and more every day now. The first days were always the most difficult ones, but things always became much better with each passing day—and before long I started to understand people more and they also showed signs that they started to understand me more. Things began to become, as people would say, more fun and more interesting.

5. Focus and stop doing anything else:

Another thing I did on top of everything else, was to concentrate exclusively on my language lesson. This is to say that whenever I started a lesson, I always finished my workout or stopped driving first. This is not to say that I did not ever listen to CDs or MP3s while on the treadmill or while driving to work, but it would be mainly to get used to the sound of a language or, at best, to maintain my listening skill of a language I have already known rather than learning a completely new language.

Chapter 6: What did I do to "unload" my extreme knowledge of French parts of speech and syntax?

As promised, I'm going to share with you, in this chapter and the next, what I did to "clean up" my knowledge of French and gain the ability to properly speak it—with ease and at the right level.

Before I start, I hope you would remember that I was a very good student in French in high school in Vietnam. With that reputation, you can imagine that I had "crammed" a lot of French grammatical concepts into my brain. Not only a lot of French parts of speech syntax and verbs but also French vocabulary. Following this reasoning, you might think that the only thing left for me to do would be to practice speaking. If things had been this straightforward, that would have been perfect. But the very fact that I had "crammed" a lot of knowledge of French into my brain while in high school ended up getting in the way of my trying to improve my French. For me to practice speaking more, therefore, I came to realize that I would need, first, to "clean up" my brain. In other words, I would need to reduce the number of things I knew before I could "recalibrate" my knowledge of French. Only after this would I be able to start re-building a solid foundation and speaking as a normal French-speaking person—and not like someone from the "upper class".

To re-build my knowledge, rather than trying to know by heart all the eight or nine parts of speech in French (some of which I realized that I did not use at all in any of my conversations), I decided to focus, now, on some of the personal subject pronouns, articles, nouns and adjectives, to begin with.

The reason why I thought, first, that I would need to know the personal subject pronouns is because I thought what I would need the most, from a grammatical perspective, is to be able to construct sentences where I could use the personal subject pronoun to say what I would like to say such as in, "Je veux…." ("I want….").

Once decided, I wrote everything down in a booklet I had bought a few days ago, as follows.

Personal subject pronouns:

First person singular:	je	("I")
Second person singular:	tu	("you")
Second person singular (polite):	vous	("you")
Third person singular:	elle, il	("she/he")
First person plural:	nous	("we")
Second person plural:	vous	("you")
Second person polite and plural:	vous	("you")
Third person plural:	ils	("they")

After the personal subject pronouns, I moved onto the articles and nouns in French. The reason why I thought I need to know the articles and nouns was because I would need to say what I would want to do as in: "Je veux envoyer un paquet…" ("I want to send a package …").

Articles:

There are two types of articles in French: indefinite and definite.

Indefinite article:

		English Equivalent
un	to be used with masculine noun that can be countable	("a/one")
une	to be used with feminine noun that can be countable	("a/one")
du	to be used with masculine noun that is uncountable	("some")
de la	to be used with feminine noun that is uncountable	("some")
de l'	to be used with feminine and masculine noun that is uncountable and starts with a vowel or whose first character sounds like a silent "h"	("some")
des	to be used only with countable noun, both masculine and	("some")

| | feminine. | |

Ex.
Un homme
("A man")
- - - -
De l'eau
("Some water")

Definite Articles:

Definite articles (le, la, l', les) are used in French when you want to refer to something more specific or to indicate the general sense of a noun.

Ex.
Le bois
("wood")

La femme
("woman")

After the articles, here is some of my notes on nouns.

Nouns:

Nouns have two genders in French: feminine and masculine. Unlike German, for instance, there is no neutral gender in French.

Ex.

Un chien
("A dog")

While most of French nouns are either masculine or feminine, some nouns, however, have a form that is the same for both feminine and masculine gender. Examples of these are: "un/une dentiste" ("a dentist").

To form the plural of a noun, we only need to add an "-s" to the ending of the noun, as in the examples below.

Ex.

Une voiture	Des voitures
("A car")	("Some cars")

The above rule being given, some nouns which end in "-eau" form the plural by adding an "-x" to the ending of the word, whereas, some other nouns which end in "-al" and "-ail", however, will form the plural by replacing those "-al" and "-ail" with "-aux" in their ending, such as in the examples below.

Ex.

Un gâteau	Des gâteaux
("A cake")	("Some cakes")

- - - -

Un cheval	Des chevaux

| ("A horse") | ("Some horses") |

The last part of speech in French I would be interested in, for this first round, is adjective.

Why adjectives you might ask?

It is because I would also like to be able to say something more qualifying such as: "Je veux envoyer un grand paquet…" ("I want to send a large package …"). Yes, a big package—not a small one.

While most French adjectives agree in gender and number with the nouns they describe, a few adjectives (the invariable ones) keep the same form for singular and plural as well as for masculine and feminine, such as in the examples below.

Ex.
Cette femme est chic
("This woman is elegant")
- - - -
"C'est un homme chic"
("This is an elegant man")

Most adjectives in French are placed after the nouns, with exceptions made of some short adjectives, which are often considered to be the intrinsic characteristic of the nouns they describe.

Ex.
C'est un beau livre

("This is a beautiful book")

In general, to make an adjective feminine, add an "-e" to the end of the adjective (unless it already ends in "-e") and to make it plural, add an "-s" to the end of the word.

Ex.
C'est une fille très intelligente
("This is a very intelligent girl")
- - - -
Ce sont des filles très intelligentes
("These are very intelligent girls")

In addition to the traditional adjectives, I also thought that I would need to know some possessive adjectives so that I could talk about something I possess or about what someone, with whom I might be speaking, possesses.

Possessive Adjectives:

The choice of which of the possessive adjectives to use in French depends on the gender of the noun being possessed, rather than the gender of the possessor. On top of this, there is an additional situation that must be assessed: whether there is one owner or whether there are multiple owners.

One owner:

English	French		
	Singular		Plural
	Feminine	Masculine	

My	Ma	Mon	Mes
Your (polite form)	Votre	Votre	Vos
Your (casual form)	Ta	Ton	Tes
His/her/its	Sa	Son	Ses

Ex.
"Ma voiture est belle"
("My car is beautiful")

Given the rule above, the reason why I wrote "Ma" instead of "Mon" was because "voiture", the thing possessed, is feminine in French and because I determined there was only one owner: me.

Many owners:

English	French		Plural
	Singular		
	Feminine	Masculine	
Our	Notre	Notre	Nos
Your	Votre	Votre	Vos
Their	Leur	Leur	Leurs
Our	Notre	Notre	Nos

Ex.
"Notre chien est fort"
("Our dog is strong")

Unlike the previous example, I used "Notre" because I determined that there were two or more owners, who were my sister and me, and because "chien" is masculine in French (though this is not clear since "notre" is used for both masculine and feminine gender).

Along with the possessive adjectives, I also thought I would need some prepositions, such as "à" ("to") or "avec" ("with") or "pour" ("for"), etc. This would, I thought, allow me to say to whom, with whom, or for whom I would be doing something, as in: "Je veux envoyer un grand paquet à mon frère…" ("I want to send a large package to my brother…").

After a few weeks of successful practice, I added direct object and indirect object pronouns, adverbs, etc. to the list. A few weeks later, I added more, again and again. For reasons of brevity, I will not produce all of them here but hope that you have understood by now what I meant when I stated in a previous chapter that "less is more."

Chapter 7: What did I do to "lower" my knowledge of French verb tenses to speak as a regular person?

You may not believe it, but even before I landed in Paris many years ago, I had already known almost all the sixteen or eighteen verbs tenses in French. Having said this, you should not be surprised to hear that rather than helping me, this got my mind crowded with so many rules and exceptions that it was difficult for me to speak French as simply and as well as I wished.

In parallel to what I did with the French parts of speech and syntax in the previous chapter, I decided that I should also find a way to "lower" my "language".

By looking at all the sixteen or eighteen tenses which I had listed on a sheet of paper in front of me, I realized that I tended to overuse both the conditional and the subjunctive tenses a bit too much. This was how I caught myself speaking during the first few months after I arrived in Paris: "Je vous serais très reconnaissant de faire savoir à monsieur que je l'attendrais aussi longtemps qu'il le souhaiterait" ("I would be much obliged if you could let milord know that I would wait for him as long as he would like me to wait") or, still, "Je ne pense pas qu'il soit d'accord avec nous" ("I do not think that he agrees with us").

Once I was convinced of this "inadequacy", I decided to "re-calibrate" my attention by focusing, first, on only the present tense, the present perfect tense, the future tense, the imperfect tense, and the pluperfect tense. You may wonder why I did not include the well-known preterit or "passé simple" in French; my answer is because it is mainly used in writing and/or in formal situations in French. I realized that the five tenses I chose to retain would be largely enough for someone like me to have decent conversations in French.

Below was what I added to my booklet on French parts of speech and syntax, right after the section on French parts of speech.

1. Present tense:

There are, in French, essentially three group of verbs which normally end in "-er", "-ir", and "-re".

Subject	Some Regular Present tense		
	-er verbs	-ir verbs	-re verbs
Singular			
	Gagner (to win)	Finir (to finish)	Descendre (to wait)
Je (I)	Gagn-e	Fin-is	Descend-s
Tu (You)	Gagn-es	Fin-is	Descend-s
Il, Elle, On (He/She/It)	Gagn-e	Fin-it	descend
Plural			
Nous (We)	Gagn-ons	Fin-issons	Descend-ons
Vous (You)	Gagn-ez	Fin-issez	Descend-ez

Ils, ells (They)	Gagn-ent	Fin-issent	Descend-ent

Ex.
Elle descend lentement de l'autobus
("She slowly gets off the bus")

Though I did not want to spend too much time on irregular verbs, below are some notes I wrote on both verbs "être" (to be") and "avoir" ("to have"), two of the most used verbs in French but which are, unfortunately, irregular.

On top of the above, the reason why I also wanted to know their present tense is because I knew that I would need to use them to conjugate the present perfect tense of the other verbs.

-"être" (to be):

	Être
Je	suis
Tu	es
Il, elle, on	est
Nous	sommes
Vous	êtes
Ils, elles	sont

Ex.
"Je suis Vietnamien mais je vis au Canada"
("I'm Vietnamese but I live in Canada")

-"avoir" ("to have"):

	Avoir
J'	ai
Tu	as
Il, elle, on	a
Nous	avons
Vous	avez
Ils, elles	ont

Ex.
"J'ai un chat mais deux chiens"
("I have a cat but two dogs")

2. Present perfect tense:

As previously said, the present perfect tense is formed by conjugating either verb "être" ("to be") or verb "avoir" ("to have") in the present tense behind which we add the past participle of the verb to be conjugated.

But before looking at one or two complete examples of the present perfect tense, I'm going to note how to form the past participle.

For regular verbs ending in "-er", to form its past participle, we only need to drop the infinitive ending "-er" before adding "é" to the stem. Some examples of this are given below.

Ex.
chanter --->chanté
("to sing")

For regular verbs ending in "-er", to form its past participle, the only thing to do is to drop the infinitive ending "-ir" before adding "i" to the stem.

For illustration purposes, an example is given below.

Ex.
mentir --->menti
("to lie")

For regular verbs ending in "-re", to form its past participle, the only thing to do is to drop the infinitive ending "-re" before adding "u" to the stem.

For illustration purposes, an example is given below.

Ex.
vendre ---> vendu
("to sell")

Now that we have seen how to form the past participle, the question that remains is: when do you use "avoir," and when do you use "être"?

Normally, the rule is to use "avoir" when it comes to a transitive verb, which requires a direct object, as in the example below.

Ex.
J'ai mangé deux pommes aujourd'hui
("I have eaten two apples today")

In other cases and especially when it comes to indicating a movement with direction, "être" ("to be") should be used.

Ex.
Elle est montée (*) pour regarder la télévision
("She went upstairs to watch TV")

(*) Note also that there is an "e" at the end of "montée". That means that the person who is speaking is of female gender. In other words, the past participle agrees with the gender of the subject when "être" is used.

3. Future tense:

To everyone's relief, the endings of the simple future tense are regular for all the verbs in French — except for both verbs "être" ("to be") and "avoir" ("to have").

To illustrate this, let's look at the endings we should add to the infinitive of the verb "parler" ("to speak").

Ex.
parler
("to speak")

	Parler
Je	parler-ai
Tu	parler-as
Il, elle, on	parler-a
Nous	parler-ons
Vous	parler-ez
Ils, elles	parler-ont

4. Imperfect tense:

Like in the case of the future tense, the endings of the imperfect tense are the same for all the verbs in French, as can be seen above — except once again for "être" and "avoir".

Let's first see how to conjugate a regular verb such as the verb "parler" ("to speak").

Ex.
parler ("to speak") :

	Parler
Je	parl-ais
Tu	parl-ais
Il, elle, on	parl-ait
Nous	parl-ions
Vous	parl-iez
Ils, elles	parl-aient

Now that we have seen how to conjugate a regular verb in the imperfect tense, let's look at the conjugation of both verbs, "être" ("to be") and "avoir" ("to have"). The reason that I wanted to spell out both "être" ("to be") and "avoir" ("to have") conjugations is because they are often used in French. We will also need them to conjugate the pluperfect tense of all the other verbs, as you will see later below.

. Être ("to be") :

	Être
Je	étais (J'étais)
Tu	étais
Il, elle, on	était
Nous	étions
Vous	étiez
Ils, elles	étaient

. Avoir ("to have"):

	Avoir
Je	avais (J'avais)
Tu	avais
Il, elle, on	avait
Nous	avions
Vous	aviez
Ils, elles	avaient

5. Pluperfect:

The same way the present perfect tense is formed by conjugating either verb "être" ("to be") or verb "avoir" ("to have") in the present tense, behind which we will add the past participle of the verb to be conjugated, what we will do for the pluperfect conjugation is conjugate either verb "être" ("to be") or verb "avoir" ("to have") in the imperfect tense, then add the past participle of the verb to be conjugated behind it. When it comes to deciding whether to use "avoir" and when to use "être," the same answer will be to use "avoir" when it comes to a transitive verb, which requires a direct object, and verb "être" ("to be") when it comes to indicating a movement with direction.

The two examples below will help clarify what we just said.

Ex.

"J'ai mangé deux pommes aujourd'hui mais j'avais mangé deux oranges hier"
("I have eaten two apples today but I had eaten two oranges yesterday")

- - - - -

"Elle est montée pour regarder la télévision il y a quelques minutes, mais son père était déjà monté dix minutes auparavant"
("She went upstairs to watch TV a few minutes ago but her father had gone upstairs for already ten minutes")

Here we are at the end of my first "re-calibration" of French verb tenses.

A few months later, I added the future perfect, the conditional present and even the subjunctive present to my list of French verb tenses to learn. For brevity's sake, I'm not going to reproduce all of them here, but you should understand by now that the lesson learned is that we should only learn what is needed, when it is needed—in a way, like in a just-in-time system.

To be honest, I was rather concerned, at first, about getting rid of so many verb tenses from my brain, which had taken me so much time to memorize while in high school. But soon, I noticed to my own delight, that people laughed less and less at how I said things. Instead, they now focused more on the content of what I was saying and took time to answer me, rather than smiling at me as some of them used to do, just a few months before.

From the above experience, I came to see how much French people are right when they say: "Il est important de savoir reculer pour mieux sauter" ("It is important to know to take a few steps back to jump further ahead.")

Chapter 8: What did I do with Spanish parts of speech and syntax when I first started to learn it?

From my previous experience with French, I decided, early on, when I started to learn Spanish that I should similarly not overload my mind with too many rules right away—unless I need them. I envisioned that, by doing that, I would not need to spend time clearing them from my head, as I had done with French grammar and verbs.

Rather than flying at ten thousand feet, let me show you tangibly what I did with Spanish so that you can see the result for yourself. To be honest, my hope in sharing some tangible examples with you here is that this will also provide you with an opportunity to see how different or close Spanish parts of speech and syntax are to French parts of speech and syntax (with both languages being part of the same Italic or Romance family). To facilitate your comparison, I will provide a French translation along with the English translation for all the examples in Spanish in the following pages.

In the same way as I had done with French, I chose not to focus on all of the eight or nine parts of speech in Spanish at once, but only instead on the personal subject pronouns as well as articles, nouns, and adjectives, to begin with. The reason why I believed I would need, first, to know the personal subject pronouns in Spanish was also because I thought what I would need the most was to be able to make a sentence like: "(Yo) quiero....." ("Je veux..."), ("I want.....").

Once decided, I went ahead and codified everything in another booklet which I bought for Spanish, as you can see below.

Personal subject pronouns:

Spanish Subject Pronoun Singular	English Equivalent
Yo	I ("Je")
Tú	You ("Tu")
Él	He ("Il")
Ella	She ("Elle")
Usted (Ud.)	you (polite) ("Vous")

Subject Pronoun Plural	English Equivalent
Nosotros (masc.)	We (Nous")
Nosotras (fem.)	We ("Nous")
Vosotros (masc.) (*Spain)	You ("Vous")
Vosotras (fem.) (*Spain)	You ("Vous")
Ellos (masc.)	They (Ils")
Ellas (fem.)	They ("Ils")
Ustedes (Uds.) (*Latin Americas)	you (polite) ("Ils")

(*) Note that people normally avoid using the second person plural familiar (vosotros, vosotras) in Latin America. Instead, they use the 3rd person plural (Ustedes, Uds.)

After the personal subject pronouns, I went onto the articles and nouns.

Articles:

Like in French, there are two types of articles in Spanish: indefinite and definite.

Indefinite articles:

Whenever we want to refer to someone or something non-specific, we use one of the following words, known as indefinite articles in Spanish: "un", "una", "unos" and "unas".

	Singular	Plural
Masculine	Un	Unos
Feminine	Una	Unas

Ex.
"Un árbol frutal"
("Un arbre fruitier")
("A fruit tree ")
- - - -
"Una mujer"
("Une femme")
("A woman")

Definite articles:

When we want to refer to someone or something specific in Spanish as in French, we need to use definite articles such as: "el", "la", "los", and "las".

	Singular	Plural
Masculine	El	Los
Feminine	La	Las

Ex.
"Sí, cocino durante el fin de semana"
("Oui, je cusine pendant la fin de semaine")
("Yes, I cook during the weekend")

Before we move onto nouns, let's note that while an article agrees with the noun in both number and gender, the exception is when it is placed in front of a feminine noun that begins with an "ah" sound as in "agua." In this case, the masculine definite article, or more precisely "el", will be needed rather than the traditional "la."

Ex.
"El agua"
("L'eau")
("The water")
- - - -
"Las aguas"
("Les eaux")
("The waters")

After the articles, we move onto (what I consider to be) the fundamentals of Spanish nouns.

Nouns:

Like in French, nouns in Spanish are either masculine or feminine.

At a high level, nouns that end in "-a" are feminine such as "casa" ("house") and "mujer" ("wife") while those that end in "-o" are masculine such as "tío" ("uncle") and "hombre" ("man").

Despite these general rules, some exceptions exist when it comes to nouns that derive from Greek which are masculine even though they end in "-a".

Ex.
"El mapa" ("The map"), "El día" (The day") or "El programa" ("The program"), etc.

This being said, all nouns that end in "-dad", "-tad", "-tud", "-ión", and "-umbre", such as "ciudad" ("city"), "universidad" ("university"), "virtud" ("virtue"), "canción" ("song") and "costumbre" ("clothing") are also feminine.

Besides this, some nouns have the same form for both gender. Examples of these are "pianista" ("pianist"), "cliente" ("client"), "dentista" ("dentist"), etc.

Now, to form the plural for nouns in Spanish, below are the rules we should follow.

For a noun of masculine gender:

We only need to add an "-s" to the nouns' ending to form the plural of a masculine noun that ends in a vowel. If the masculine noun ends in a consonant, then we should add "-es" instead.

Ex.

"Un amigo"	"Unos amigos"
("Un ami")	("Des amis")
("A friend")	("Some friends")

- - - -

"Un animal"	"Unos animales"
("Un animal")	("Des animaux")
("An animal")	("Some animals")

For a noun of feminine gender:

Normally, we only need to add an "-s" to the nouns' ending to form the plural of a feminine noun that ends in a vowel. If the feminine noun ends in a consonant, then you should add "-es" instead.

Ex.

"L'agua"	"Las aguas"
("L'eau")	("Les eaux")
("Water")	("Some waters")

- - - -

"Una ciudad"	"Unas ciudades"
("Une cité")	("Des cités")
("A town")	("Some towns")

When speaking a language such as Spanish or French, it is important to know the gender of the noun, as in French, because that will determine the form of article, type of pronoun, or ending of the adjective which describes it, etc.

The next Spanish part of speech that I was interested in, for the first few weeks, was the adjective.

Adjectives:

In Spanish, as in French, adjectives must also agree with the noun they accompany or describe in both gender and number.

Ex.
"Es una señora rica"
("C'est une femme riche")
("It is a rich woman")

Most adjectives in Spanish are generally placed after the nouns, except when it comes to short adjectives, which are often considered to be the intrinsic characteristic of the nouns they describe.

Ex.
"Yo soy una joven doctora"

("Je suis une jeune doctoresse")
("I'm a young female doctor")

In the example above, "doctora" ("doctoresse"), ("doctor") is the noun and "joven" ("jeune"), ("young") is the adjective that is used to indicate that the doctor is a young person.

Before moving onto the possessive adjectives, I noted that some adjectives would lose their "-o" when they precede a masculine singular noun, as in the example below.

Ex.
"Mi hermano es un buen obrero"
("Mon frère est un bon ouvrier")
("My brother is a good blue collar worker")

But if these adjectives follow the noun, then they will retain the usual ending, meaning without losing the "-o". The example below is given to clarify this point.

Ex.
"Mi hermano pequeño"
("Mon jeune frère")
("My little brother")

To form the plural for adjectives, we only need to add an "-s" to the ending of the adjective, as in the example below.

Ex.
"Las cocinas extranjeras"
("Les cusines étrangères")

("The foreign cuisines")

As previously mentioned, the final part of speech I thought I would need in Spanish was the possessive pronouns.

There are two sets of possessive adjectives in Spanish: one is called "the long form" (which is the equivalent of the English "of mine", "of hers", etc.), and the other is called "the short form" (which is the equivalent of "my", "his" in English, etc.).

Either way, the possessive adjectives must agree in gender and number with the thing possessed — and not the possessor.

But, for the need that I had at the beginning, I was interested in the short forms, hence my note in the table below.

English equivalent	Spanish Possessive adjectives
My	Mi, mis
Your (informal)	Tu, tus
His/her/your (polite singular)	Su, sus
Our	Nuestro, nuestros/ nuestra, nuestras
Your	Vuestro, vuestros/ vuestra, vuestras (Spain) suyo, suyos/suya, suyas (Latin Americas)
Their (max., fem.), your	Su, sus

(polite plural)	

Ex.
"¿Qué acerca de tu casa?"
("Quoi à propos de ta maison?")
("How about your house?")

To use my Spanish possessive adjectives, I thought, again, that I would need to at least know some prepositions, such as "a" ("à"), ("to") or "con" ("avec"), ("with") or "por" ("pour"), ("for"), etc.

This was for me to be able to say to whom, with whom, or for whom I would be doing something, such as: "(Yo) quiero enviar un paquete grande a mi hermano" ("Je veux envoyer un grand paquet à mon frère…"), ("I want to send a large package to my brother…").

I hope by now that you have seen what I considered, at the time, to be the fundamentals of what I would need from Spanish grammar, to begin with. At the same time, I hope you have also seen the difference or, rather, the similarity between French and Spanish parts of speech and syntax—and why knowing one could also help me, or anyone else for that matter, to learn the other.

Now that we're done looking at French and Spanish parts of speech and syntax, I'm going to, in the next chapter, share with you what I thought I would need in terms of verb tenses in Spanish for my upcoming trip to Spain. Unlike what I had done with French, where the goal was to simplify my hyper-theoretical knowledge of French, the goal this time was to build up my Spanish knowledge. Going back to my upcoming trip to Spain, some of you might wonder what this trip was for? To keep things more interesting and you in suspense, let me only say, for now, that it was a trip for my company's business. This said, I promise you that I will reveal, after the next chapter, all the details as to how exactly the trip came about and what I was planning on doing during the trip. Likewise, I will also share with you why, after the trip, I became able to speak Spanish so well for such a long time thereafter, while not practicing all too often.

Chapter 9: What else did I do to my list of Spanish verb tenses before I took the first flight to Spain?

Following what I did to successfully "re-calibrate" my French, if you guess that I would just do the same with Spanish, then you have guessed wrong. The reason for this is the need I had to travel to Spain for my company. For fear of not looking as polished as someone who would represent corporate headquarters, I added both the preterit and the conditional present tenses to the list of the verb tenses I had to know before I left for Spain.

Like in French, all verb conjugations in Spanish are grouped around a few categories. More specifically, there are three groups of conjugations in Spanish, which respectively end in "-ar", "-er" and "-ir".

Let's now review each tense, one by one, to see how we conjugate verbs in Spanish.

1. Present tense:

"- ar":

Below is an example of the present tense of "cocinar" ("to cook").

Ex.

"cocinar" - - - - > stem: "cocin-

("to cook")

	cocin-ar
Yo	cocin-o
Tú	cocin-as
Usted (Ud.)	cocin-a
Él/Ella	cocin-a
Nosotros/as	cocin-amos
Vosotros/as (Spain)	cocin-áis
Ustedes (Uds.) (Latin Americas)	cocin-an
Ellos/Ellas	cocin-an

Ex.
¿Cocinas, cierto?
("Tu cusines, n'est-ce pas?")
("You cook, right?")

"-er":

Below is an example of the present tense of "saber" ("to know"):

Ex.
"saber" - - - - > stem: "sab-"
("to know")

	sab-er
Yo	sé
Tú	sab-es
Usted (Ud.)	sab-e

Él/Ella	sab-e
Nosotros/as	sab-emos
Vosotros/as (Spain)	sab-éis
Ustedes (Uds.) (Latin Americas)	sab-en
Ellos/Ellas	sab-en

Ex.

"Mis amigos no saben cómo cocinar"
("Mes amis ne savent pas comment cusiner")
("My friends do not know how to cook")

"-ir":

Below is an example of the present tense of "vivir" ("to live").

Ex.
vivir " - - - - > stem: "viv-"
("to live")

	viv-ir
Yo	viv-o
Tú	viv-es
Usted (Ud.)	viv-e
Él/Ella	viv-e
Nosotros/as	viv-imos
Vosotros/as (Spain)	viv-ís
Ustedes (Uds.)	viv-en

(Latin Americas)	
Ellos/Ellas	viv-en

Ex.

"Soy de Chile pero vivo en Francia"
("Je suis du Chili mais vis en France")
("I'm from Chile but I live in France")

2. Present perfect tense:

Like in French, the present perfect tense is formed in Spanish by conjugating the verb "haber" ("avoir"), ("to have") or the verb "ser" ("être"), ("to be") in the present tense, at the end of which we must add the past participle of the main verb to be conjugated.

Before we look at some examples of the present perfect, let's see how we form the past participle of regular Spanish verbs first. To do this, simply drop the infinitive ending before adding "ado" for verbs ending in "ar" or "ido" for verbs ending in "er-" and "ir".

To illustrate the above, an example is given below.

- cantar --------> cant-ado,
- beber --------> beb-ido

Now, let's look at the present perfect of comprar ("to buy").

From the rule given above, this would mean something like:

Present tense of "haber" + past participle of "comprar" (= "compr-ado")

But, before we look at that, let's look first at the present of "haber" ("to have")

	haber
Yo	he
Tú	has
Usted (Ud.)	ha
Él/Ella	ha
Nosotros/as	hemos
Vosotros/as (Spain)	habéis
Ustedes (Uds.) (Latin Americas)	han
Ellos/Ellas	han

Now, if we put together the present perfect of "haber" and the past participle of "comprar" ("to buy"), then below is what we would get:

	comprar
Yo	he comprado
Tú	has comprado
Usted (Ud.)	ha comprado

Él/Ella	ha comprado
Nosotros/as	hemos comprado
Vosotros/as (Spain)	habéis comprado
Ustedes (Uds.) (Latin Americas)	han comprado
Ellos/Ellas	han comprado

Ex.
"He comprado un vehículo"
("J'ai acheté un véhicule")
("I have bought a car")

3. Future tense:

After the present perfect tense, here is my note on the future tense.

The good news here is that all of the endings for the future tense are the same for all three conjugation groups: "-é", "-ás", "-á", "-emos", "-éis", "-án". The only thing left would be to add them to the verb infinitive, as can be seen in the examples below.

"-ar":

"comprar"
("to buy")

	comprar
Yo	comprar-é
Tú	comprar-ás
Usted (Ud.)	comprar-á
Él/Ella	comprar-á
Nosotros/as	comprar-emos
Vosotros/as (Spain)	comprar-éis
Ustedes (Uds.) (Latin Americas)	comprar-án
Ellos/Ellas	comprar-án

Ex.

"Compraré el carro mañana para ir a la universidad
("J'acheterai la voiture demain pour aller à l'université »)
("I will buy the car tomorrow to go to the university")

"-er":

"comer":
("to eat")

	comer
Yo	comer-é
Tú	comer-ás
Usted (Ud.)	comer-á
Él/Ella	comer-á
Nosotros/as	comer-emos
Vosotros/as (Spain)	comer-éis
Ustedes (Uds.)	comer-án

(Latin Americas)	
Ellos/Ellas	comer-án

Ex.
"Comeremos juntos en un buen restaurante la próxima semana"
("Nous mangerons emsemble dans un bon restaurant la semaine prochaine")
("We will eat at a good restaurant next week")

"-ir":

"vivir"
("to live")

	vivir
Yo	vivir-é
Tú	vivir-ás
Usted (Ud.)	vivir-á
Él/Ella	vivir-á
Nosotros/as	vivir-emos
Vosotros/as (Spain)	vivir-éis
Ustedes (Uds.) (Latin Americas)	vivir-án
Ellos/Ellas	vivir-án

Ex.
"Viviré con mucho placer en España"
("Je vivrai avec beaucoup de plaisir en Espagne")
("I will live with a lot of pleasure in Spain")

4. Imperfect tense:

Simply put, below are the conjugation rules for "-ar", "-er" and "-ir" regular verbs for the imperfect tense.

"-ar":

"comprar" ---------> stem: "compr-"
("to buy")

	compr-ar
Yo	compr-aba
Tú	compr-abas
Usted (Ud.)	compr-aba
Él/Ella	compr-aba
Nosotros/as	compr-ábamos
Vosotros/as (Spain)	compr-abais
Ustedes (Uds.) (Latin Americas)	compr-aban
Ellos/Ellas	compr-aban

Ex.
"Mi hermana compraba una casa grande cada año
("Ma sœur achetait une grande maison chaque année")
("My sister bought a big house every year")

"-er":

"comer" ---------> stem: "com-"
("to eat")

	com-er
Yo	com-ía
Tú	com-ías
Usted (Ud.)	com-ía
Él/Ella	com-ía
Nosotros/as	com-íamos
Vosotros/as (Spain)	com-íais
Ustedes (Uds.) (Latin Americas)	com-ían
Ellos/Ellas	com-ían

Ex.
"A veces comía el pescado"
("je mangeais parfois du poisson")
("Sometimes I ate fish")

"-ir":

"vivir" ---------> stem: "viv-"
("to live")

	viv-ir
Yo	viv-ía
Tú	viv-ías
Usted (Ud.)	viv-ía
Él/Ella	viv-ía
Nosotros/as	viv-íamos
Vosotros/as (Spain)	viv-íais
Ustedes (Uds.) (Latin Americas)	viv-ían

| Ellos/Ellas | viv-ían |

Ex.
"(Yo) jugaba fútbol todos los sábados"
("Je jouais au football tous les samedis")
("I used to play soccer every Saturday")

To help us know when the imperfect tense will be needed in Spanish, below are some words or expressions that would help us realize that the imperfect would be needed: "a veces" ("parfois"), ("sometimes"), "cada día" ("chaque jour"), ("each day"), "en el pasado" ("dans le passé"), ("in the past"), "normalement" ("normalement"), ("normally"), "todos los sábados" ("tous les samedis"), ("every Saturday"), "generalmente" ("généralement"), ("generally"), "a menudo" ("souvent"), ("often"), "siempre" ("toujours"), ("always"), etc.

There you go. Above is where I should have stopped, had I not needed to travel to Spain.

Below are the two additional tenses I added.

5. Preterit tense:

Whenever we want to talk about an action in Spanish that occurred and was completed at a specific time in the past, we need to use the preterit tense.

Below are the conjugation rules for "-ar", "-er" and "-ir" regular verbs in the imperfect tense.

For verbs ending in "-ar", simply drop "-ar" from the infinitive and add the following endings:

yo	-é
tú	-aste
él/ella/Ud.	-ó
nosotros	-amos
vosotros	-asteis
ellos/ellas/Uds.	-aron

Applying the above rule, following is the result you will get for:

"-ar":

"comprar" ---------> stem: "compr-"
("to buy")

	compr-ar
Yo	compr-é
Tú	compr-aste
Usted (Ud.)	compr-ó
Él/Ella	compr-ó
Nosotros/as	compr-amos
Vosotros/as (Spain)	compr-asteis
Ustedes (Uds.) (Latin Americas)	compr-aron

| Ellos/Ellas | compr-aron |

Ex.
"Compré un carro ayer"
("J'achetai une voiture hier")
("I bought a car yesterday")

For verbs ending in "-er" and "-ir", simply drop "-er" and "-ir" from the infinitive and add the following endings:

yo	-í
tú	-iste
él/ella/Ud.	-ió
nosotros	-imos
vosotros	-isteis
ellos/ellas/Uds.	-ieron

Applying the above rule, the following is the result you will get
for:

"-er":

"comer": ---------> stem: "com-"
("to eat")

	com-er
Yo	com-í
Tú	com-iste
Usted (Ud.)	com-ió
Él/Ella	com-ió

Nosotros/as	com-imos
Vosotros/as (Spain)	com-isteis
Ustedes (Uds.) (Latin Americas)	com-ieron
Ellos/Ellas	com-ieron

Ex.
"Comí con una amiga ayer"
("Je mangai avec une amie hier")
("I ate with a female friend yesterday")

As in the case of the imperfect tense, below are some words or expressions that would help us realize that the preterit tense will be needed in Spanish: "ayer" ("hier"), ("yesterday"), "el otro día" ("l'autre jour"), ("the other day"), "la semana pasada" ("la semaine dernière"), ("last week"), "un día" (un jour"), ("one day"), "una vez" ("une fois"), ("one time"), "de repente" ("soudainement"), ("suddenly"), "anoche" ("hier soir"), ("last night"), "anteayer" ("avant hier"), ("the day before yesterday"), etc.

To help determine how to use the imperfect tense and when to use the preterit tense, I added the example below.

Ex.
"Mientras hablaba con tu hermano, me llamaste"
("Pendant que je parlais avec ton frère, tu m'appellas")
("While I was speaking with your brother, you called me")

6. Conditional present tense:

The good news with the conditional tense in Spanish is that the same endings "-ía", "-ías", "-ía", "-ía", "-íamos", "-íais," and "-ían" are to be added, as in the table below, to the verb stem, regardless of whether it belongs to the "-ar", "-er," or "-ir" group.

"-ir": "vivir", drop "ir" -------> stem: "viv-"
("to live")

	viv-ir
Yo	vivir-ía
Tú	vivir-ías
Usted (Ud.)	vivir-ía
Él/Ella	vivir-ía
Nosotros/as	vivir-íamos
Vosotros/as (Spain)	vivir-íais
Ustedes (Uds.) (Latin Americas)	vivir-ían
Ellos/Ellas	vivir-ían

Ex.

"Viviría en Nueva York si tuviera un poco más de dinero"
("Je vivrais à New York si j'avais un peu plus d'argent")
("I would live in New York if I had a little bit more money")

Here we are at the end of what I did with Spanish verb tenses. I think you should have seen by now how Spanish fundamentals are not that difficult and how close, at a high level, they are to French.

In the next chapter, I'm going to share with you, as promised, how my trip to Spain came about, what it was for, and why I became so good at speaking Spanish for many years thereafter—or, as some would say, almost never forget it. This is a subject we will look at in more detail towards the end of the book.

Chapter 10: What are the two things I also did that helped me be comfortable speaking Spanish for such a long time thereafter?

When this was taking place, I was working as a manager for an international conglomerate. Not being satisfied with speaking Spanish with people alone, I decided one day that I should give a training session in Spanish to some of our software teams from Spain. Being a manager who was responsible for software development methodology at the time, I thought that would make a good subject for my class. Believing that I had found a good idea, I prepared a proposal which I quickly submitted to our head of corporate IT, who to my own delight, approved it almost immediately. Without wanting to get into the nitty-gritty details of corporate politics, the official reason I got for why my proposal was approved was, first, because spreading the right software development practice to the IT organization was my responsibility and, second, because top management liked the idea of having one of theirs travel to another country and give a class in one of the European languages. For them, it would show how much we, at the corporate headquarters, understood and cared about our differences in languages and cultures.

From a rather small action item I took to mainly improve my Spanish to "sharing" software development best practices to the rest of the IT organization in Spain, I suddenly realized that this had become a corporate initiative—the success of which I would want everyone and myself to be proud.

Given the fact that I had already had some solid foundation in Spanish, I wrote up some imaginary conversations between two friends to start practicing by myself. There is a total of more than 15 conversations, but for reasons of brevity, I will only reproduce a few below for illustration purposes.

Lesson 1: Exchanging greetings between friends

[Estudiante 1] Hola.
[Estudiante 2] Hola.
[Estudiante 1] ¿Cómo estás?
[Estudiante 2] Estoy bien, gracias. ¿Y tu?
[Estudiante 1] Estoy bien, gracias.
[Estudiante 2] Es una hermosa mañana.
[Estudiante 1] Sí, es una hermosa mañana.
[Estudiante 2] Y, va a durar todo el día

[student 1] Good morning.
[student 2] Good morning.
[student 1] How are you doing?
[student 2] I'm fine, thanks. And you?
[student 1] I'm fine, thanks.
[student 2] It is a beautiful morning.
[student 1] Yes, it is a beautiful morning.
[student 2] And, it is going to last the whole day.

Lesson 2: Inquiring about a friend's birthday

[Estudiante 1] ¿Cuál es tu cumpleaños?
[Estudiante 2] El Seis de febrero. ¿Cuál es tu

                   cumpleaños?
[Estudiante 1] Ocho de marzo.
[Estudiante 2] Es pronto.
[Estudiante 1] Sí, es pronto.
[Estudiante 2] ¡Qué suerte!
[Estudiante 1] Gracias.
[Estudiante 2] De nada.

[student 1] What is your birthday?
[student 2] February Sixth. What is your birthday?
[student 1] Eighth of March.
[student 2] It is soon.
[student 1] Yes, it is soon.
[student 2] How lucky!
[student 1] Thanks.
[student 2] You are welcome.

Two weeks after reading aloud the conversations to myself while acting as if I was two friends speaking with one another, I started to feel even more confident about speaking in Spanish.

The above being said, the thought of having to spend eight hours or more per day in Spain, surrounded by people whose main language is Spanish, made me feel somewhat concerned. One thing I realized that would enable me to not have to speak all the time was to know how to ask people questions. This way, I thought, I could balance them out, speaking and listening—both of which are important to me. Once I made up my mind, I decided that the best way would be for me to only know one or two of the most used ways to ask questions in Spanish. The first way, I found out, was to add "¿verdad?" ("n'est-ce pas?"), ("right?") to the end of the sentence, as in: "¿Trabajas aquí, verdad?" ("Travailles-tu ici, n'est-ce pas?"), ("You work here, right?"). The second way was to invert the subject and the conjugated verbs as in: "¿Estás de acuerdo conmigo?" ("Es-tu d'accord avec moi?"), ("Do you agree with me?").

After internalizing the course material a few times, which was the Spanish translation of one hundred slides or so and which I had personally written in French, I took the flight to Valencia in Spain. To my own delight, not only did our Spanish colleagues like the idea of having a foreigner come to give them a class in their mother tongue, but also welcomed me as "one of them," as they were delighted to see that I only wanted to speak Spanish. Yes, only in Spanish, with nearly no word in French nor in English (knowing that English was our company's official language for all official communications between different business units).

As I took a deep breath doing my teachings, I was so glad that everything went well. After that successful two-day class and a lot of conversations, I was invited to fly back to Spain some more times to either advise or work with our Spanish teams, this time not only from Valencia (where I flew to originally), but also from Barcelona and Madrid. Due to our bonding, my Spanish friends would, every time, shower me with gifts. Once, they even put money together to buy me an expensive watch as a gift. Another time, which I still remember as if it were yesterday, some of my colleagues from Spain bought me two sticks of chorizo, almost one foot long each, gifting them to me just before I left for the airport. When I arrived at security at the airport, I was somewhat concerned that they would inspect my luggage and, as luck would have it, they did. When the customs officer saw my two long chorizo sticks, rather than taking them back and reprimanding me, he smiled and suggested that next time I should ask for some more as Spain has a variety of great chorizos. While I was trying to say how much I appreciated his advice, he kindly signaled for me to move forward.

So, now you know what two things I did with Spanish that created a multiple of improvements which, altogether, helped dramatically improve my ability to speak Spanish for a long time to come. It is as if, beyond a certain threshold, all the things I did—from looking up new words in the dictionary, to creating conversations in Spanish, to reading them every day, to drafting grammar and verb summaries, and to practicing speaking Spanish—during a condensed period collided together to create an explosive effect on the brain that made it easy for me to easily recognize the sound of Spanish and be able to speak it at any time thereafter.

From my story above, my suggestion is that, if you are learning a new language, you should try not only to practice speaking, but if possible, also try to look for an opportunity to give a class—as I did—or take part in a play in the new target language, to further immerse yourself.

Now, to go back to the training I gave in Spain. I know, in hindsight, that I must have made some mistakes in Spanish during those two days of training. Looking back many years later, it still makes me smile thinking about it. But my Spanish colleagues, in their kindness, never wanted at the time to make me realize that I had said something wrong. At least, that is how I think they thought. How would I know that I had made some mistakes in Spanish during that two-day class that I taught? I know because during the many times that I would come back to some of the very sentences I had previously said and attempt to correct them, my Spanish colleagues would invariably say "sí" to me with a smile, implying that they understood what I was now trying to correct, even if previously they had also said "sí" ("yes"), implying that they had agreed with or at least understood me when I initially said those sentences the first time. So, despite two "sí"' and a few smiles, I knew that somewhere along the way I had confused them with some badly formulated sentences in Spanish, but being friendly, they likely said to themselves, "Never mind. The guy is trying to be friendly by speaking with us in our mother tongue. Let's give him a break."

Inspired by the "good ambience," I went on successfully teaching my class. What did I learn from this experience? Not that I was smart, but that I had found a way to communicate with my colleagues from Spain in their own language, which not only helped me dramatically increase my ability to speak Spanish but also led our colleagues from Spain to want to work even more closely with the corporate headquarters, which I represented at the time.

Now, to now go back to the two verb tenses I added to the original list, my effort, as I had hoped, largely paid off. By the end of that week in Spain, I counted that I had used the conditional tense no less than 20 times and the subjunctive tense no less than 15 times—both inside and outside of the class room. With this, it became clearer to me than ever before that we should not learn grammar and verbs systematically or all at the same time, but let our need determine what portion of the grammar and verb tenses we should learn and when we should learn them.

While my above statement might sound a little bit obvious, you may be surprised by how much grammar and how many verbs people are still required today to learn even before they can say one single sentence in the new target language.

By looking at what I did during all those years, I could see why I was effective at language learning. It was not because I was smart or because I was particularly good at languages. For me, it was because I was not only excited to learn but also looked forward to putting the result of my learning into practice as soon as possible. These are the reasons why, no matter what languages I chose to learn, I always learned with passion and intensity.

Despite the above success, I observed that it still took me, at the time, several months to a year or two to learn and be fluent in a new language. While this fact did not bother me too much at first, it did make me wonder at times how I could learn a new language in much less time. Even though there was no emergency, I nonetheless believe that the seed was planted then. More on this later.

Chapter 11: Which foreign languages of what family of languages should you learn to speak first?

You may remember me mentioning the phrase "family of languages" in speaking about French and Spanish in a previous chapter. This said, you have not yet been formally introduced to them as to know what they really are. This is why I'm going to more formally talk to you about them here, in this chapter, to give you an idea of what they are and what kinds of benefits you can expect by learning languages of the same family.

By introducing you to the concept of family of languages here, I also hope that it will help you better understand some of the reasons why I was successful at learning Italian in three weeks, which I will outline in the next chapter.

Without further ado, let's now review what the main families of languages are:

While there are hundreds of languages around the world, many of the most known are grouped around more than a dozen families of languages; these include: Indo-European, Sino-Tibetan, Austro-Asiatic, Indo-Aryan, Austronesian, Afro-Asiatic, Uralic, Niger-Congo, Altaic, etc.

For illustrative purposes, below is the list of some of the often-mentioned languages that are known to be part of the above families of languages (without counting the subfamilies in between):

1.Indo-European:		
	Germanic:	Swedish, Norwegian, Danish, Icelandic, German, Yiddish, Dutch, Flemish, English, Afrikaans, etc.
	Italic:	Italian, French, Romanian, Spanish, Catalan, Portuguese, Corsican, Sardinian, etc.
	Celtic:	Welsh, Irish, Breton, etc.
	Slavic:	Russian, Serbian, Ukrainian, Polish, Czech, etc.

	Hellenic:	Greek, Macedonian, etc.
2.Sino-Tibetan:		Chinese, Tibetan, etc.
3.Austro-Asiatic:		Vietnamese, Khmer, etc.
4.Indo-Aryan:		Hindi, Bengali, Punjabi, Burmese, Nepalese, etc.
5.Austronesian:		Tagalog, Malay, Indonesian, etc.
6.Afro-Asiatic:		Arabic, Hebrew, Ethiopian, Ancient Egyptian, etc.

7.Uralic:		Hungarian, Finnish, Estonian, etc.
8.Niger-Congo:		Swahili, Yoruba, Shona, etc.
9. Altaic:		Japanese, Korean, Mongolian, Turkish, etc.

By providing the list above, I do not intend to recommend that you learn foreign languages only by their families. That would take away all the fun. But if the idea of learning a new language by leveraging a language you have already learned within the same family is something that interests you, then I think the list above would be helpful to you.

Rather than focusing mainly on cognates as the main, if not the only, benefit of learning languages within the same family, I'm going to broaden this "common heritage" between languages within the same family by talking not only about cognates, but also about parts of speech and syntax.

I have previously shared with you a comparison between French and Spanish parts of speech and syntax, but in case you are still not too familiar with French, I'm going to show you below a comparison between Spanish and Portuguese parts of speech and syntax. Besides sharing more knowledge with you, this is also to make sure that you see that this is not just a coincidence.

First, we will look at the parts of speech, then we will review the cognates together.

1. Comparison between Spanish and Portuguese parts of speech and syntax:

Before we look at syntax, meaning how people build sentences or negate sentences in Spanish and Portuguese, let's first look at their parts of speech.

Indefinite articles:

Spanish	Portuguese	English Equivalent
un	um	a / an (masculine)
una	uma	a / an (feminine)
unos	uns	some (masc. plural)
unas	umas	some (fem. plural)

Demonstrative adjectives:

Spanish	Portuguese	English Equivalent
este	este	this (masculine)
esta	êsta	this (feminine)
estos	êstes	these (masculine)
estas	êstas	these (feminine)
ese	êsse	that (masculine)
esa	êssa	that (feminine)
esos	êsses	those (masculine)
esas	êssas	those (feminine)

Demonstrative pronouns:

Spanish	Portuguese	English Equivalent
éste	êste	this (masculine)
ésta	êsta	this (feminine)
éstos	êstes	these (masculine)
éstas	êstas	these (feminine)
ése	êsse	that (masculine)
ésa	êssa	that (feminine)
ésos	êsses	those (masculine)
ésas	êssas	those (feminine)

As you can see, there is quite a bit of similarity between Spanish and Portuguese parts of speech here.

Next, after their parts of speech, below is how a sentence would look like in both Spanish and Portuguese.

"Mis padres viven in Nueva York"
"Meus pais vivem em Nova York"

("My parents live in New York")
- - - -
"Soy frances pero vivo en los Estados Unidos"
"Sou francês mas vivo nos EUA"
("I'm French but I live in the USA")

And, now, let's look at how a negative sentence would look like in both Spanish and Portuguese.

Ex.
"No he bebido jamás el vino"
"Eu tenho bebido jamais o vinho"
("I have never drunk wine")
- - - -
"Sí, cocino durante el fin de semana"
"Sim, eu cozinho durante o fim de semana"
("Yes, I cook during the weekend")

Without saying that they are identical, word for word, I think you would agree that Spanish and Portuguese parts of speech and syntax look very similar.

Now that we are done looking at some parts of speech and syntax between Portuguese and Spanish, let's look at cognates. In addition to examining cognates between Spanish and Portuguese, we will also look at cognates between English and German, between English and French, and finally, between English and Spanish.

2. Cognates:

2.1 Cognates between Italic languages:

Cognates between Spanish and Portuguese:

Words that end in "-ción" in Spanish will usually end in "-ção" in Portuguese.

Ex.

Constalación	Constelação
Construción	Construção

Words that end in "-ible" in Spanish usually end in "-ível" in Portuguese.

Ex.

Possible	Possível
Terrible	Terrível

Words that end in "-nía" in Spanish usually end in "-nia" Portuguese.
Ex.

Agonía	Agonia
Autonomía	Autonomia

As previously stated, let's now look at the cognates within the Germanic family first.

2.2 Cognates within the Germanic languages:

Cognates between English and German:

Words which end in "-ion" in English usually end the same in German.

Ex.

Immigration	Immigration
Information	Information

Words which end in "-y" in English usually end in "-ie" in German.

Ex.

Battery	Batterie
Theory	Theorie

Words which end in "-ort" in English usually end the same in German.

Ex.

Export	Export
Import	Import

Words which end in "-ent" in English usually end the same in German.

Ex.

Instrument	Instrument
Moment	Moment

Words which end in "-al" in English usually end the same in German.

Ex.

International	International
Irrational	Irrational

Words which end in "-or" in English usually end the same in German (with the "h" in English sometimes omitted).

Ex.

Author	Autor
Professor	Professor

Words which end in "-ct" in English usually end in "-kt" in German.

Ex.

Indirect	Indirekt
Perfect	Perfekt

2.3 Cognates within the larger Indo-European family:

- Cognates between English and French:

Words which end in "-al" in English are usually the same in French.

Ex.

Final	Final
Original	Original

Words which end in "-ary" in English usually end in "-aire" in French.

Ex.

| Dictionary | Dictionnaire |
| Salary | Salaire |

Words which end in "-ant" in English usually end the same in French.

Ex.

| Distant | Distant |
| Tolerant | Tolerant |

Words which end in "-tion" in English generally have the same ending in French.

Ex.

| Bastion | Bastion |
| Conversation | Conversation |

Words which end in "-ent" in English usually end the same in French.

Ex.

| President | President |
| Monument | Monument |

Words which end in "-ble" in English usually end the same in French.

Ex.

| Possible | Possible |
| Terrible | Terrible |

- Cognates between English and Spanish:

Words which end in "tion" in English end in "-ción" in Spanish.

Ex.

| Direction | Dirección |
| Construction | Construcción |

Words which end in "-ble" in English usually end the same in Spanish.

Ex.

| Cable | Cable |
| Terrible | Terrible |

Words which end in "-ant" in English usually end in "-ante" in Spanish.

Ex.

| Important | Importante |
| Distant | Distante |

Words which end in "-ly" and sometimes in "-ely" in English usually end in "-mente" or "-amente" in Spanish.

Ex.

| Finally | Finalmente |
| Directly | Directamente |

Words which end in "-id" in English change to "-ido" in Spanish.

Ex.

Valid	Válido
Lucid	Lúcido

Here we are at the end of this chapter on families of languages.

Even with all the examples above, I do not mean to imply that knowing a language of the same family as the new language you want to learn will be enough to make your learning an automatic success. However, with everything else being equal, it will be certainly a big help if you know how to leverage your previous knowledge of another language of the same family.

Chapter 12: How to build up your Russian, Arabic, Swahili, Chinese, and Japanese vocabulary fast?

You may have been delighted to see that there are so many cognates between English and many of the Italic and Germanic languages. This said, you may wonder what to do if the new language you're learning is not of the same family as one of the languages you have already learned.

Having observed people (including myself, many years back) painstakingly learn new vocabulary, word by word, my goal here is to share with you a few strategies that I discovered to build up vocabulary for a new language quickly—regardless of whether it is of the same family as one of the languages you have already learned or not.

Without overloading you with the linguistic terms for these techniques, I'm going to share three of them which you can use to quickly build up new vocabulary. The first one (1) is by analyzing word roots; the second one (2) is by looking at words under influence; and finally, the third one (3) is by looking at the words upon which the new words are built (word combination).

Let's review them one by one below.

1. Words by root analysis:

As I had mentioned above, we will look at the root system in some languages such as in Russian and Arabic.

- Russian root system:

To better help you understand how the root system works in Russian, let me, first, say that there is what we call the root and, then, there is what we call either a prefix or a suffix.

Rather than losing you with lengthy explanations, let's look at some examples below for illustrative purposes.

Assuming first that there is "ход", a root which means something like "movement."

Next, if we add "в", a prefix which means something like "in" before the root, we will then get "вход", which would mean something like a "movement into something" or "entrance" in Russian.

To continue with the same root, let's imagine that we add a different prefix—the prefix "вы́" (which means something like "out" in Russian)—to the root. We will then get "вы́ход", which would mean something like a "movement out of something" or "exit" in Russian.

Now, let's imagine that we add yet another prefix— the prefix "у" (which means "away")—to the same root "ход". We will then get "ухо́д", which would mean a "movement away from something" or "escape" in Russian.

Just as we have done with prefixes, we can also use suffixes to create new words in Russian. Below are some examples for you to look at.

To begin, let's assume that we have another root – the root "уче", which means "to learn" in Russian.

Now if we add a suffix—the suffix "-ник", which means something like "a male"—behind the root "уче", we get "ученик", which means "a male student" in Russian.

Parallel to "-ник", if we now use another suffix—the suffix "-ница"—and add it to the root "уче", we will then get "ученица", which means "a female student."

To continue our examples with suffixes, let's now imagine that we have another root—the root "учи", which means "to teach" in Russian.

Now, if we have a suffix "-тель" and add it behind the root "учи", we will then get "учитель", which means "a male teacher" in Russian.

When one single root in Russian, combined with either prefixes or suffixes, can produce up to 90 new words on average, you can see how many new words you would be able to learn or guess the meaning of, if you knew even 30 roots: around 2,700 new words or so, which should largely be enough for you to speak with people or even read a newspaper or, better yet, Leo Tolstoy's or Fyodor Dostoyevsky's famous classics.

- Arabic root system:

Like the Russian root system, Modern Standard Arabic (MSA) has also a system based on what people call the three core letters, from which a multitude of nouns and adjectives are derived.

To begin with, let's take the three letters "k", "t," and "b" (ك ت ب) as part of the verb "to write", "كَتَبَ" or "kataba" in Arabic transliteration. From this verb and the three letters (k-t-b) it contains, you can easily see or guess that "kitaab" is a book; "mktab", an office; "maktabah", a library; "katīb", a writer; and "maktubī", a bookdealer, etc.

To ensure that it is not just a coincidence, let's now look at another three letters "J", "M," and "L", which, in Arabic, stands for everything that relates to beauty. From this, you could easily see or guess that "jamal" is beautiful; "tajmil", beautification; "mujaamala", a compliment, etc.

I know that I had previously said that whatever language you would want to learn is up to you; but with regards to Arabic, I would suggest that you first learn Modern Standard Arabic (MSA) if you're not interested in any specific North African or Middle Eastern country's dialect.

In case you might not know, MSA is one of the six official languages of the United Nations and is spoken by more than 400 million people in the Islamic world. Knowing how to speak it will enable you to understand and be understood by many people in many countries across the Middle East and North Africa. Once you've got a good knowledge of

MSA, learning a regional Arabic dialect should be a rather easy undertaking.

Beyond the above, another thing that I found very interesting is the fact that knowing Modern Standard Arabic could also help you quickly build up your vocabulary in Swahili, one of the most beautiful languages from Africa. As many other languages such as Turkish, Urdu, Bengali, Hindi, Malay, etc. that were greatly influenced by Arabic, Swahili is also known to be influenced by Arabic from which it borrows many words for its vocabulary.

If Swahili is new to you, it is a language spoken by around 80 million people across countries such as Tanzania, Kenya, Congo, Burundi, Rwanda, Uganda, etc. So, if you happen to travel to one of these countries, just imagine how much the people there would be delighted to see you speak their language.

As mentioned above and to show you an example of Arabic influence on Swahili, below is a short list of Swahili words that come from Arabic:

Swahili	Arabic	English
ada	adā	fee, payment
alama	alāma	mark, symbol
asali	ʻasal	honey, syrup
baraka	baraka	blessing
bila	bilā	without
dawa	dawā	remedy
falaki	falak	astrology
imla	imlā	spelling

Etc.	Etc.	Etc.

2. Words under influence:

Now that we have spent some time on root analysis, let's look at some more examples of words next that may have been influenced by another language, such as Greek over French or English, and French over English and Vietnamese.

Let's assume for the moment that you know Greek. If this is the case, then you should be able to guess what the word "agonie" in French means since you know that its root word "agonie" comes from the Greek word "Agonia," meaning "the last fight" or "la dernière lutte."

Likewise, you should be able to also guess the meaning of the French word "diamant" if you know that its root comes from the Greek word "adamas," meaning "pure hard rock" or "la pierre la plus pure et dure." And if you know the Greek word "acouo", which means something related to "sound," then you should be able to deduct or guess that the French word "acoustique" should mean something related to "sound."

Likewise, if you know the word "armonia", which means "good accord" in Greek, then you should have no difficulty in guessing that the French word "harmonie" would mean something harmonious.

In the same way, if you know the two Greek words "pro," meaning "promoting," and "biotic," meaning "life", then you should be able to guess the English word "probiotic" as something helpful to life.

Lastly, you should also be able to guess that "hématie" in France has something to do with blood or the study of blood since its root comes from the word "aïma," which means "blood" in Greek.

Now that we have reviewed some more of the influence of Greek over French and English, let's look at some of the influence of Latin over French and English.

For this, let's assume that if you know that "Litigum" in Latin means dispute or disagreement, then you should be able to guess that "litigation" in English would mean something like "a dispute."

In this same way, you should be able to deduct that "metropolitan" in English would mean something like "a city with a diverse population" since that is what "metropolis" means in Latin.

Finally, let's now look at the influence of French over both English and Vietnamese.

Not too many people know that after the successful conquest of England by the French Duke of Normandy around 1066 AD, French remained the main language of the English upper classes for the next two hundred years.

This is to say that if you know French, then you could guess that the English word "constitution" would mean the same thing as the French word "constitution," the highest legal document of a country.

Likewise, if you know the French word "converse", meaning dialogue, then you should be able to guess that the English word "conversation" would mean something like a dialogue as in French.

France also used to govern Vietnam for almost one hundred years a few centuries ago. During this colonial time, the French left their mark on the Vietnamese language, such as in the examples below.

Ex.
"xúc xích" in Vietnamese comes from the French word "sausage" ("sausage")

"kem" in Vietnamese comes from the French word "crème" ("cream")

"bê tông" in Vietnamese comes from the French word "béton" ("concrete")

"vi ô long" in Vietnamese comes from the French word "violon" ("violin")

"cà phê" in Vietnamese comes from the French word "café" ("coffee") "gác" in Vietnamese comes from the French word "garde" ("guard")

"búp bế" in Vietnamese comes from the French word "poupée" ("doll")

"ban công" in Vietnamese comes from the French word "balcon" ("balcony")

"cao su" in Vietnamese comes from the French word "caoutchouc" ("rubber").

3. Words combination:

Now, in order to see how you would be able to build up a new set of vocabulary by looking at the word foundation, let's look at some examples of Chinese words and see for ourselves how many words in Chinese are, in effect, built on top of other words.

Ex.

cài: dish; vegetable
chăng: place

- - - - -> càichăng: vegetable market

- - - -

cài: dish; vegetable
dāo: knife

- - - - -> càidāo: kitchen knife

- - - - -

wén: word
zhōng: middle

- - - - -> zhōngwén: Chinese literature

- - - - -

wén: word
xué: study

- - - - -> wénxué: literature,

etc.

xué: to study
xiǎo: small

- - - - -> xiǎoxué: elementary school

- - - - - - - -

xué: to study
zhōng: middle

- - - - -> zhōngxué: middle school

- - - - - -

xué: to study
dà: middle

- - - - - -> dàxué: college/university

- - - - - - - -

zì: letter/symbol/character
  mǔ: mother

- - - - -> zìmǔ: letter

- - - - - - - -

zì: letter/symbol/character
  jì: trace

- - - - -> zìjì: handwriting

- - - - -

qiān: sign, tag, label
zì: letter/symbol/character

- - - - -> qiānzì: signature.

- - - - -

chéng: city
mén: gate

- - - - -> chéngmén: city gate

- - - - -
chéng: city
qū: area

- - - - -> chéngqū: urban area; district

The same way you had learned about some great Arabic influence on Swahili, Chinese also has some great influence on Japanese in that a large portion of the Japanese vocabulary comes from Chinese, known as "Chinese words" or "kanji". "Kanji" is one of the three components of the Japanese language, with the other two components being "hiragana" (representing the very basic Japanese phonetic script) and "katakana" (representing Japanese words that are imported from foreign languages.)

To give you an idea of the influence of Chinese over Japanese, below are some examples of "kanji" in Japanese that are borrowed from Chinese.

Japanese	Chinese	English
人	人	Person
山	山	Mountains
日	日	Sun
生	生	Life
Etc.	Etc.	Etc.

Even though the sound of both Japanese and Chinese is different from the sound of Vietnamese and of all the Western languages I had learned, I find Japanese and Chinese sound to be both very beautiful, and two very interesting languages to learn and to speak.

Here we are at the end of this chapter on how quickly you can build up a new vocabulary. The same way I had cautioned you not to overload your brain with too much grammar before you need it, I will caution you here also not to overload your brain with too much vocabulary and all at once. While everyone is different but on average I will recommend that you learn only between fifteen and twenty new words per day.

Chapter 13: What did I do to learn to speak Italian in three and a half weeks?

Among all the Italic or Romance languages I know, while I find French elegant, Spanish convivial, and Portuguese quite exotic, I'm particularly impressed by the sound of the Italian language, which I find to be very attractive. This is the reason why I'm not surprised that people usually choose Italian to sing Opera. This said, Italian is also the only language which I didn't have an opportunity to really learn.

So, upon hearing that our children had come together to buy my wife and me tickets for a one week of vacation in Rome as a birthday gift, I told myself that this may be the opportunity I needed to learn Italian and make the trip as fun as possible.

Since I have walked you through a comparison of French and Spanish parts of speech and syntax, I will spare you the same with Italian since they are luckily rather similar. Instead, I will share with you what I found out about Italian and English cognates and what verb tenses I decided this time around to learn, and why. Likewise, I will also share with you what I did with the conversations, which I believe helped dramatically reduce the time it took me to learn a new language, Italian in this case, to only three and a half weeks.

Let's first look at the cognates.

A. English and Italian cognates:

Words which end in "-tion" in English usually become "-zione" in Italian.

Ex.

Liberation	Liberazione
Lotion	Lozione

Words which end in '-or' in English usually become "-ore" in Italian.

Ex.

Motor	Motore
Professor	Professore

Words which end in - ty usually become "-tà" in Italian.

Ex.

City	Città
Verity	Verità

Words which end in "-ary" in English usually become "-ario" in Italian.

Ex.

Necessary	Necessario
Adversary	Avversario

Words which end in "-ic" in English usually become "-ico" in Italian.

Ex.

Domestic	Domestico
Majestic	Majestico

Words which end in "-ly" in English usually become "-mente" in Italian.

Ex.

Exactly	Esattamente
Mentally	Mentalmente

Words which end in "-ous" in English usually become "-oso" in Italian.

Ex.

Delicious	Delizioso
Vicious	Vizioso

Words which end in "- al" in English usually become "-ale" in Italian.

Ex.

Local	Locale
National	Nazionale

Words which end in "-ment" in English usually become "-mento" in Italian.

Ex.

Movement	Movimento
Pigment	Pigmento

B. Italian verb tenses:

As previously mentioned, below is a summary of the Italian verb tenses that I chose to learn for the trip: (1) the present tense, (2) the present perfect tense, and (3) the future tense.

By looking at the tenses above, you might wonder why only these three tenses? If you think that is because of the short trip, you would be right – but only half right. The other reason why I chose to learn only three tenses for my trip to Italy is because I had observed after many years that people usually use the present, future present perfect tense, or the imperfect tense for most of their conversation needs. Let's assume that all the 16 verb tenses combined represent 100% of our conversational needs, this would mean as if we would only need 20% of the verb tenses for 80% of our conversational needs.

Now, to go back to the verb tenses I thought I would need for this one-week trip to Italy, the reason why I did not retain the imperfect tense was because I envisioned that I would not have much to say to our Italian friends about any past events that I would have shared together with them.

The other thing I decided on was to find some ways that would allow me to quickly engage in conversations without having to bother to conjugate any verbs. From my previous trips to Spain, I remembered hearing people say things like: "Me gusta…" ("I like to…."), behind which the verb would stay in the infinitive form. As this form was quite practical, I decided to do some research to see if people in Italy also had something similar or not. To my delight, I found that they had a phrase which went like: "Mi piace…." ("I like to …"), the equivalent of what I had heard during my different trips to Spain. Glad to have found something as practical as that in Italian, I hurriedly wrote it down on a sheet of paper to remember.

Now that we have discussed the reason why I chose the above tenses to learn and seen what I did with "Mi piace…" ("I want to…"), let's review the verb tenses themselves, one by one.

1. Present tense:

Verbs ending in "-are".

Parlare ("to speak"). Drop the stem "-are" and add "-o", "-I", "-a", "-iamo", "-ate", "-ano".

Ex.
"comprare" ("to buy")

compr	
-o	(io)
-i	(tu)
-a	(lui, lei)
-iamo	(noi)
-ate	(voi)
-ano	(loro)

Verbs ending in "-ere". Drop "-ere" before adding "-o", "-i", "-e", "-iamo", "-ete", "-ono".

Ex.
"correre" ("to run") prendere ("to take")

corr-o	prend-o
corr-i	prend-i
corr-e	prend-e
corr-iamo	prend-iamo
corr-ete	prend-ete
corr-ono	prend-ono

Verbs ending in "-ire" like aprire ("to open") or partire ("to leave").

Verbs ending in "-ire" like in aprire.

Ex.
"aprire" ("open")

apr-o	apriamo
apr-i	aprite
apr-e	aprono

2. Present perfect tense:

This tense is formed by the present tense of the auxiliary verb ("avere" or "essere"), behind which we add the past participle of the verb to be conjugated.

Now, how do we know whether we should conjugate with "avere" or "essere"? We will use "avere" when it comes to a transitive verb that requires a direct object and "essere" when it comes to an action or movement verbs that do not require a direct object.

How about creating the "past participle"? It is formed by replacing the infinitive endings with the following endings:

- and(are)   : "and-" + ("ato") for verb ending in "-are"
- av(ere)   : "aver-" + ("uto") for verb ending in "-ere"
- dormire   : "dorm-" + ("ito") for verb ending in "-ire"
- conoscere   : "conosc-" + ("iuto") for verbs ending in "-scere".

Present perfect with "avere":

	Avere	
(io)	ho	lavorato
(tu)	hai	lavorato
(lei/lui/Lei)	ha	lavorato
noi	abbiamo	lavorato
voi	avete	lavorato
loro/Loro	hanno	lavorato

Ex.
"Abbiamo lavorato tutto il giorno prima di andare al cinema"
("Hemos trabajado todo el día antes de ir al cine")
("We have worked the whole day before going to the movies")

Present perfect with "essere":

	Essere	
(io)	sono	arrivato/a
(tu)	sei	arrivato/a
(lei/lui/Lei)	è	arrivato/a
noi	siamo	arrivati/e
voi	siete	arrivati/e
loro/Loro	sono	arrivati/e

Ex.

"I miei genitori sono arrivati a casa ieri"
("Mis padres han llegado a casa ayer")
("My parents have arrived home yesterday")

3. Future tense:

Change the "-are" and "-ere" infinitive endings to "-er-", and drop the final "-" from "-ire" verbs. After this, add:

io	-ò
tu	-ai
lui/lei	-à
noi	-emo
voi	-ete
loro/Loro	-anno

Here we are, at the end of my selection of Italian verb tenses to learn for my trip to Rome.

Given the short time I had to learn Italian before our trip, I said to myself that I should quickly find some Italian speakers with whom to practice. This said, fearing that it would not be enough if I went through these conversations only once, I then decided that I should have the native speakers record the conversations, giving me time to take part in them to re-listen to "see" if I could recognize my own sentences and understand the conversations in their entirety.

As luck would have it, I handily found two students who were available at that exact timeframe to help me with whatever I needed at a rather reasonable cost. Sensing the opportunity, I decided that rather than using only the 15 original conversations I had previously created for Spanish, we should not only adapt and translate them into Italian but also add another set of 25 new conversations, all in Italian, to the list as part of a "story line". By "story line", what I mean is that rather than having many conversations that do not share any connection between one another, my conversations would be written in such a way that they are more interwoven with one another—in such a way that they should be able to provide the overall story line or language context to my learning.

After three weeks of listening-repeating-conversing-recording-replaying on repeat, I started to feel that I would soon be ready to speak with people face-to-face in Italian. It was then that I decided the time had arrived for me to go to Little Italy to practice.

As always, the visit to the first Italian restaurant was the most difficult one. But determined to get as much practice as possible, I returned to Little Italy over the course of the next two weeks. After a few times, I became more relaxed as new sentences came more easily out of my mouth. With each passing day, I felt more and more comfortable speaking Italian. By the third week, I felt like I had been speaking Italian for already quite some time.

Just to give you an idea of how seriously I was studying Italian prior to our trip to Italy, two days before our departure I took out a sheet of paper to write a short note in Italian to some imaginary people with whom I envisioned that I had been speaking during the past two and a half weeks. Below is the entire text in Italian along with its English translation for you to review and enjoy.

Buonasera à tutti

Poichè oggi è l'ultima volta che ci incontriamo, ho scritto un testo breve che mi piacerebbe leggervi per ricordare le nostre conversazioni e per condividere i miei sentimenti.

Primo, anche se è stato solo un breve periodo di tre settimane più o meno, è stato uno dei ricordi più belli della mia vita.

Per di più, l'italiano è una delle lingue più belle che mi piacciono molto ma che non ho avuto l'opportunità di parlare formalmente con un gruppo di amici tanti gentili come voi.

Allora, di tutti i paesi che ho visitato, e ne ho

visitati molti, Italia è stata uno dei più belli paesi a cui ho sempre voluto andare ma non ci sono ancora andato.

Spero che dopo qualche preparazione io riesca a sentirmi abbastanza confidente nella mia conoscenza d'Italia e dell'italiano per visitare Italia e soprattutto parlare con la gente.

Infine, ho letto molto su Italia nelle tre settimane scorse e mi sono reso conto che gli italiani hanno una cultura diversa ed elegante.

Ecco in pochi parole i miei sentimenti a proposito del tempo che abbiamo scorso parlando insieme.

Grazie e molti auguri à tutti!

Un amico

- - - - -

Good evening everyone

Because today is the last time we will meet, I have written a short text which I would like to read to you all to mark our conversations and to share my feelings.

First, despite that this is only a short period of around three weeks, it has been one of the best memories of my life.

Second, Italian is one of the most beautiful languages, which I love but had not had the

opportunity to formally practice with a group of friends as nice as you all.

Third, out of the many countries I have visited, and I have visited many, Italy may be probably one of the most beautiful countries which I have always wanted to visit but which I have not yet visited until now.

I hope that, after this preparation, I'm going to feel more confident in my knowledge of Italy and of Italian to think of visiting Italy where I wish to discuss everything with people.

Finally, I have read a lot about Italy during these three weeks and have realized that the Italians have a very diverse and elegant culture.

There you have it, in a few words, my feelings for the time we have spent discussing things together.

Thank you and best wishes to all!

A friend

It would not be completely true to say that I had expected to speak Italian as smoothly as I did during my vacation to Italy with my wife. But the truth is that everything I said, from the minute we landed to the minute we left for the airport to fly back to New York, was entirely in Italian. This is something which caught my wife off guard—to her delight and surprise, as she said.

To be even more precise, not only did I try to speak in Italian but I also "refused" to speak in any language other than in Italian. To better illustrate what I mean, let me share with you an anecdote that happened one day when my wife and I were wandering around the Quirinal Palace (one of the three official residences of the president of the Italian Republic). After ten or fifteen minutes in the area, my wife wondered how to get to the Fontana di Trevi. Not knowing how to get there, I approached the presidential guard in front of the building and asked him: "Fontana di Trevi?"

To which he replied: "Go down there and straight on your right…."

Deciding to converse only in Italian, I said: "In Italiano, per piacere." ("In Italian, please.")

With a smile, he responded back: "Scusi. Scendete e dritto sulla destra..." ("Sorry. Go down and straight on the right…")

I then said: "Mille grazie." ("Thank you.")

To which he said with a large friendly smile: "Prego. Benvenuti a Italia e buona giornata." ("No problem. Welcome to Italy and have a good day.")

Now you know what I mean when I said that I really meant to speak Italian in Italy. "When in Rome, do like the Romans," so goes the popular saying.

Along with what I did at the Quirinal Palace with the presidential guard, I also even "refused" to speak in any language other than Italian back at the restaurant of the hotel where we were staying. Unbeknownst to us at first, we came to realize a day or two later that I had touched the headwaiter so much by speaking with him in Italian that he made it a point to serve us as if we were some kinds of special guests in a classic movie inside the famous Grand Hotel. Not just one day but every day during breakfast, he would drop by our table, asking us if we would like to try this or that dish, which he, then, would personally bring to our table. When you know that all the meals were part of the price of our hotel stay which had been already paid for by our children, you could guess why I believe what the headwaiter did come from some personal feeling for some tourists who spoke with him in his mother tongue rather than because he was driven by some extra sale.

Even though I had been somewhat ambivalent at first about spending one week in Italy (not knowing if I would be able to learn Italian fast to be ready in three weeks), but as it turned out, my wife and I had one of the best times of our life in Italy—first in Rome, next in Florence, then back to Rome.

On the learning side, delighted by my success in learning Italian in barely three and a half weeks, I thought it would be interesting to put all the conversations along with the grammar stuffs in a safe place for future reference. At the same time, I also thought that it would be time to create a template for the grammar and verbs summary I created for Italian to reuse with all the languages I would like to learn, going forward.

To give you a complete picture of what they are, below is, first, the list of the 40 conversations, and, next, the layout of the grammar and verbs template.

Lesson 1: Exchanging greetings between friends

Lesson 2: Inquiring about a friend's birthday

Lesson 3: Telling a friend about your family

Lesson 4: Talking about one another family's house

Lesson 5: Cooking or ordering in?

Lesson 6: Asking about the outside of the house

Lesson 7: Talking about sports

Lesson 8: Cooking at home or eating out

Lesson 9: Talking about going to the movies

Lesson 10: Talking about one another's work schedule

Lesson 11: Going to the shopping mall

Lesson 12: Do you have some other friends in town

Lesson 13: What about going on vacation together

Lesson 14: How should we go on vacation together

Lesson 15: Inquiring about the weather at the beach

Lesson 16: How about having lunch together?

Lesson 17: How about dropping by the chocolate shop?

Lesson 18: How about going to the flowers market now?

Lesson 19: How about going to the fair?

Lesson 20: Why not have a picnic in the countryside

Lesson 21: Why not stop for lunch on the road?

Lesson 22: Do you know how to play piano?

Lesson 23: Have you ever tried yoga?

Lesson 24: Is there a post office nearby?

Lesson 25: I'm having an appointment with my doctor

Lesson 26: How about going to the zoo?

Lesson 27: Admiring animals at the zoo

Lesson 28: How about going to a concert?

Lesson 29: How about going for a walk in the park?

Lesson 30: What about having dinner together?

Lesson 31: How about dropping by a bookstore?

Lesson 32: Talking about an upcoming birthday

Lesson 33: How was the meal?

Lesson 34: Booking a trip online

Lesson 35: Preparing the baggage

Lesson 36: Are you at the airport yet?

Lesson 37: Have you landed yet?

Lesson 38: Arriving at the hotel

Lesson 39: What time to wake up tomorrow morning?

Lesson 40: Visiting museums on spare time during the trip

- - - - -

Essence of Grammar and Verbs

Introduction

Types of sentences

Positive sentences

Active sentences
    Interrogative sentences
    Passive sentences
    Commanding sentences

Negative sentences

Review of the different parts of speech

Nouns

Pronouns
    Personal subject pronouns
    Direct object pronouns
    Indirect object pronouns

Articles
    Indefinite articles
    Definite articles

Adjectives
    Variable adjectives

Adverbs
    Adverbs of quantity
    Adverbs of manner

Prepositions

Conjunctions
                Coordinating conjunctions

Interjections

Verbs

        Impersonal verbs/expressions
        Present indicative tense
        Future indicative tense
        Present perfect indicative tense

Numerical

Cardinal numbers

Cognates (words with similar spelling and meaning)

Despite the fact that I was excited by the result of my Italian learning, I somewhat tempered my excitement by deciding that I should try to test my method again with another language to see if it would yield the same result. What I did not know at the time was that the next language I was going to use to test my new method would be Chinese Mandarin. This is what I am going to share with you in the next chapter.

Chapter 14: How did I learn to speak Mandarin Chinese in four weeks?

To be honest, I was somewhat at a loss when I first decided to learn Chinese. I had no pointer to refer to as I had had with other Western languages. So, the first thing I did was to go to a bookstore, hoping to find some books to read more about Chinese. It was during this time that I learned about the existence of Pinyin or the westernization of Chinese letters. As soon as I found out about this, I quickly dropped my intent to learn Chinese by using a character-based approach. The reason for this was, I guess, because that would also require me to have to learn to read and, probably, to write at the same time. That, in my mind, would require a lot more effort and take me too long.

Adopted by the Beijing government in 1958, Pinyin has become the standard around the world for foreigners who want to learn to speak Mandarin Chinese. What this means is that rather than having to learn characters such as the following: 他吃汉堡包, we can, instead, use the following western-alphabet based Pinyin words: "Tā chī hànbǎobāo" ("He eats hamburgers"), with "Tā" being the transcript of "他", "chī" the transcript of "吃" and "hànbǎobāo" being the transcript of "汉堡包".

In Pinyin Chinese, there are 6 vowels (a, o, e, i, u, ü) and 21 consonants (b,p, m, f, d, t, n, l, g, k, h, j, q, x, zh, ch, sh, r, z, c, s.)

While most of the consonants are easy to pronounce, somewhat like in the West, one of the trickiest sounds to pronounce correctly in Mandarin for English speakers is the "r" sound as in "rén" ("person"). Luckily, for those of us who know French, this "r" should be pronounced like "j" in "jour" ("day") or "journal" ("newspaper") in French.

Like the consonants, Chinese vowels are also easy to pronounce, except maybe the "ü", which should be pronounced like the German "umlaut" as in "über."

Besides the above observations, with so many words in Chinese Pinyin having the same spelling, it is clear that some tones need to be differentiated between words with the same spelling. This explains why tones are of vital importance in Mandarin Chinese. In total, there are five tones in Mandarin, four of which are shown in the table below (since there is no sign for the fifth one).

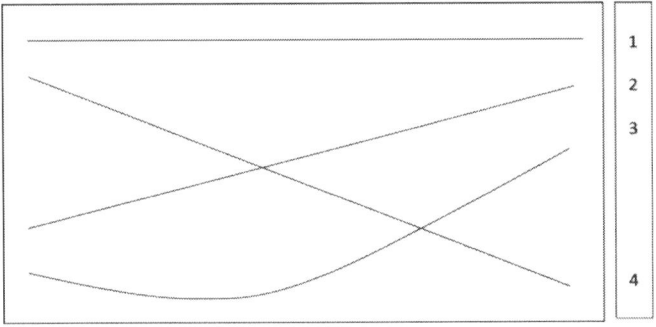

First Tone: ¯

This tone is designated by a straight line over the vowel (as in "mā" for "mother" in English and is pronounced high and remains steady like the "a" in "far".

Second Tone: ´
This tone's symbol is an upward slant from right to left over the vowel (as in "má" for "hemp" in English or for "mother" in Vietnamese) and begins rather low in the mid-tone then rises to a high tone.

Third Tone: ˇ
This tone, known as the falling tone, starts low then goes even lower before rising to a high tone (as in "mǎ" for "horse" in English or as in "mã" for "tomb" in Vietnamese).

Fourth Tone: `
This tone is represented by a downward slant from right to left over the vowel (as in "mà" for "to swear") and begins in a high tone but falls sharply at the end like as in "mà!" for a polite way to say an order in Vietnamese.

Fifth Tone:
There is no sign for this one. You will find example of this in words such as "ma" for "ghost" in Vietnamese or as in "ma" in Chinese, which is used to form a question.

Ex.
"Nǐ hǎo ma?"
("How are you?")

Believe it or not, when you separate learning to read and write from learning to speak, Chinese suddenly looks much easier than English.

The above being said, let me share with you what I did for my summary of Chinese grammar and verb tenses—using practically the same template I had used with Italian.

1. Parts of speech in Chinese:

As we talked about at length in addressing the Indo-European languages, let's look at the parts of speech in Chinese. You will be surprised to see that in Chinese there are what are called parts of speech and they may be sometimes even simpler than they can be in Italic or Italic languages.

Let's review them one by one below:

Pronoun:

Words used to refer to either people or things. There is in Chinese no distinction between subject pronouns and object pronouns. Wǒ (I/me), nǐ (you), nín (you, polite) tà (he/him, she/her, it/it), wǒmen (we), nǐmen (you, plural), tàmen (they/them, plural), etc.

Ex.
Wǒ dǒng
I understand
(Wǒ: I; dǒng: understand)
----

tā gěi wǒ sān běn shū
He gives me three books

Qǐng bié dòng tā!
Please do not touch it!

Nouns:

Same concept as in English, but one good thing to note is that there is no change in the noun spelling, even when pluralizing.

Ex.
xuéshēng
student/students

----

yínháng
bank/banks

While the above represents the majority of cases with nouns, some exceptions do exist where we will be required to add "mén" to behind the noun in singular to create a noun in plural, as in the examples below.

Ex.

xiānsheng	xiānsheng mén
gentleman	gentlemen

péngyǒu	péngyǒu mén
friend	friends

Articles:

Unlike English, there is no such thing as "a", "an," or "the" in Chinese.

Ex.
háizimen xǐhuān nǐ
The children like you
(háizimen: children; xǐhuān: like; nǐ: you)

----

zhège yǒu wèntí
this has a problem
(zhège yǒu: This has; wèntí: problem)

Adjectives:

In Chinese, if the adjective is pronounced with only one syllable, then it should be placed directly in front of the noun it describes, just like "lǜ" ("green") in the example below.

Ex.
wǒ hē lǜ chá
I drink green tea
(wǒ: I; he: drink; lǜ: green; chá: tea)

If the adjective has more than two syllables, you will need to add a possessive particle "de" between it and whatever noun it describes.

Ex.
zhèshì yīge jiǎndān de wèntí
this is a simple question

(zhèshì: This is; jiǎndiān: simple; de: possessive particle; wèntí: question)

Adverbs:

hěn (very), yě (also), hū rán (suddenly), etc.

Ex.
zhège hěn hǎo
this is very good
(Zhèige: This is; hěn: very; hǎo: good)

Preposition:

dào (to), cóng (from), wǎng (forward), etc.

Ex.
wǒ zài zhǎo wǒde péngyǒu
I'm looking for my friends
(wǒ: I; zài: a word that indicates an action in progress, the equivalent of "am" in the example above; zhǎo: to look for; wǒde: my; péngyǒu: friend)

Classifier:

In Chinese whenever you want to specify a quantity for a noun, you must use what is called a measure word. There are over a hundred of them, but the most often used are: gè (often to be used as a general measure word or with people), bēi (to be used with items such as cups of tea or coffee), běn (to be used with objects such as books and magazines), bǎ (to be used with objects with handles such as chairs, knifes, umbrellas, toothbrushes), kuài (to be used with cakes), jiàn (to be used with clothing), tái (to be used with large electrical machines), zhī (to be used with cigars or cigarettes), and jiā (to be used with shops, hospital or restaurants), etc.

Ex.
Wǔ ge érzi
Five sons
----
sān bēi kāfēi
Three cups of coffee

Zhè běn shū bù shì wǒ-de
This book is not mine

Now that we have gone through a short review of Chinese parts of speech, let's look at what I did to learn all of the key Chinese verb tenses—in about two days.

2. Chinese verb tenses:

There are three types of verbs in Chinese: non-action, action and modal verbs. By non-action verbs, I mean verbs that denote ideas or state of things such as "xǐhuān" ("to like"), "dǒng" ("to understand"), "ài" ("to love"), wèn ("to ask"), etc. By action verbs, I mean verbs such as "kànshū" ("to read a book"), qù ("to go"), "chī" (to eat), etc. By modal verbs, I mean verbs that precede action verbs such as "yào" ("to want to do something"), "néng" ("to be able to do something"), "huì" ("to know how to do something"), "xiǎngyào" ("to like to do something"), "yīnggāi" (should do something), etc.

When it comes to Chinese verb conjugation, the first thing to note, with a sign of relief, is that Chinese verbs do not change endings — regardless of person or number.

This being said, let's look at the conjugation for the various tenses in Chinese now.

2.1 Present tense: The same for both non-action and action verbs.

Ex.
Wǒ kànshū
I read/am reading a book

Wǒ qù xuéxiào
I go to school

If we want to emphasize the fact that we are doing something right at this moment, we must add either "zài" before the verb or "ne" after the verb or even both at the same time.

Ex.
Wǒ zài kànshū
I'm reading a book right at this moment

Wǒ kànshū ne
I'm reading a book

Now, if we want to emphasize something with a "no-action" verb, we must add "shì" before the verb.

Ex.
Wǒ shì xǐhuān tā
I do like him

2.2 Present perfect tense:

There are three ways we can describe in Chinese an action that started in the past but which was completed in the present time.

a.   Guò... le

verb + guò (+object) + le   or   verb + guò (+object)

Ex.
Nǐ chī guò fàn le ma?
Have you eaten yet?

Nǐ qù guò zhōngguó ma?
Have you been to China?

b.   Le...le

verb + le + object + le   or   verb + le + duration phrase + le

Ex.
Wǒ kàn le nà běn shū le
I've read that book

----

xiǎo Wáng zǒu le sān tiān le
Mr. Wǎng has been gone for 3 days

2.3 Future tense:

A peculiarity in Chinese is that we can also use the present tense to describe something that will take place in the future. The only thing to do is to add some time expressions such as "míngtiàn" ("tomorrow") or "měitiàn" (every day) to before the verb as in the examples below.

Ex.
Tā míngtiān hē chá
He will drink tea tomorrow

However, if we want to emphasize that something will only take place in the future, we must add either "yào" or "huì" in front of the verb.

Ex.
Tā míngnián huì dào Fǎguó qù
He will go to France next year

2.4 Past tense:

The main difference between "non-action" verbs and "action" verbs when it comes to past tense is that we will need to add the "le" particle by the end of the sentence with an action verb.

Ex.

tā zuótiān qù xuéxiào le
He went to school yesterday
(tā: He; zuótiān: yesterday; qù: to go; xuéxiào: school; le: an indicator of past action)

Note, however, that we should never add the "le" particle to a "non-action" verb to describe an idea from the past.

Ex.

Tā xǐhuān wǒ
He liked me

The same way as with the future tense, if we want now to emphasize an idea from the past, we must add "shì" to before the "non-action" verb as in the example below.

Ex.
Wǒ yǐqián shì xǐhuān tā
I did like him before

2.5 Conditional:

When it comes to the conditional, there are many ways to say this but I only retained these two:

Yàoshi...jiù   If …., then…
Rúguǒ...jiù   If …., then…

Ex.
Yàoshi tā qù, wǒ jiù qù
If he goes, then I will go

Rúguǒ tā qù, wǒ jiù qù
In case he goes, then I will go

3. How to create an active sentence in Chinese Mandarin?

In English, a main sentence structure is written like this: Subject + Predicate (Verb and Complement). Surprisingly enough, while there is such a structure in Chinese, there are also some other sentence structures as well. All in all, we can say that there are four or five most frequently used ways to structure a sentence in Chinese:

3.1 Subject-verb-object

3.2 Subject-time and/or location

3.3 Time-Subject-Verb

3.4 Topic-Subject-Verb-Time and/or Location:

3.5 Subject-Preposition-Verb-Object.

Let's review these, one by one, with the examples below.

3.1 Subject-verb-object:

At the very basic level, a sentence in Mandarin will have the same structure as a basic English sentence, meaning the subject precedes the predicate as in the example below.

Ex.

Tā chī hànbǎobāo
He eats hamburgers
(Tā: He; chì:eats; hànbǎobào: hamburgers)

Wǒ xiǎng qǐng nǐ chī fàn
I want to invite you to eat
(Wǒ: I; xiǎng: like; qǐng: invite; nǐ:you; chì fàn: to eat)

3.2   Subject-time and location:

In this type of structure, both the time and location must be placed before the verb but behind the subject pronoun. Otherwise, when both location and time are in the same sentence, the time must be placed before both the location and the verb.

Ex.
tā wǔ diǎn zài kànshū
He was reading a book at 5 o'clock
(tā: he; wǔ: five; diǎn: o'clock; kànshū: read)

----

tā zài jiā kànshū
(tā: He; zài: at; jiā: home; kànshū: read a book)

----

tā wǔ diǎn zài jiā kànshū
He was reading a book at 5 o'clock at home
(tā:He; wǔ:five; diǎn: o'clock; zài: at; jiā: home; kànshū: read a book)

3.3 Time-Subject-Verb:

Ex.

zuótiān wǒ zài kànshū
Yesterday, I read a book at home
(zuótiān: yesterday; wǒ: I; zài: at; jiā: home; kànshū: read a book)

3.4 Topic-Subject-Verb-Time and/or Location:

Ex.
Zhège zhōngwén diànyǐng, wǒmen zuótiān zài jiā dōu kàn guò
This Chinese movie, we have already watched at home
(zhège zhōngwén diànyǐng: This Chinese movie; wǒmen: we; zuótiān: yesterday; zài: at; jiā: home; dōu kàn guò: have watched [with guò indicating a completed past action])

3.5 Subject-Preposition-Verb-Object:

In this type of structure, the subject comes first, then the "indirect object," then the verb tense, and finally, the direct object.

Ex.
Mama wèi wǒ mǎi-le yí ge diànnǎo
Mother bought me a computer
(Mama: My mother; wèi wǒ: for me; mǎi-le: bought with le indicating a past action; yí ge diànnǎo: a computer [with ge as a measure word for large object such as a computer])
----
wǒ gēn wǒde péngyou shuō
I speak with my friends
(wǒ: I; gēn: with; wǒde péngyou: my friends; shuō: speak)

Now that you have seen the fundamentals of Chinese parts of speech and verb tenses, below is what I wrote about how to create a negative sentence and how to form an interrogative sentence in Chinese. The reason I put them here is because it would have been difficult to understand them before we look at the parts of speech and verb tenses.

4. How to create a negative sentence in Chinese Mandarin?

In Chinese, there are three main ways to create or turn a positive sentence into a negative sentence. First (1), by using "bù", second (2), by using "méi", and third (3), by using "bié".

Let's review them, one by one.

4.1 Using "bù": to essentially build a negative sentence in the present and future tenses as in the example below.

Ex.
Wǒ bú kàn diànshì
I do not watch TV
(Wǒ: I; bú: the negation word; kàn: watch; diànshì: TV)

4.2 Using "méi": we have just seen how to use "bú" to build a negative sentence, but when it comes to negating a sentence with the verb "yǒu" ("to have"), we must use "méi" instead, placing it right before "yǒu", as in the example below.

Ex.
tā méi yǒu qián
He does not have money
(tā: He; méiyǒu: does not have; qián: money)

Similarly, we will also need to use "méi" to negate a past action, as can be seen in the example below.

Ex.
tā zuótiān méi kàn diànshì
He did not watch TV yesterday
(Tà: He; zuótiān: yesterday; méi kàn: did not watch; diànshì:TV)

4.3 Using "bié": whenever you would like to say a strong suggestion or an order to someone.

Ex.
Bié kàn diànshì!
Don't watch TV!
(Bié: Don't; kàn: watch; diànshì: TV)

5. How to form an interrogative sentence in Chinese?

The first and simplest way is (1) to add "ma" by the end of the sentence without switching the order between the subject and the verb, as in the example below. The second way is (2) to use an interrogative word such as "shénme" or "mǎr" when it comes to a question about a direct object or location.

Ex.

Nī shuō zhōngwén ma?
Do you speak Chinese?
(Nī: You; shuō: speak; zhōngwén: Chinese; ma: serving as a question mark)

Ex.
Use an interrogative word such as "shénme" or "năr":

Nĭ hē shénme?
What do you drink?
(Nĭ: You; hē: drink; shénme: what)

In creating the above summary, I came to realize how much Chinese grammar and verbs were much simpler than that of most Western languages. With this new discovery, I decided that I should focus on vocabulary building, from now on. It was in building my new Chinese vocabulary that I was led to discover how Chinese people build many new words by combining existing ones together, something I had shared with you a few chapters back.

Given the first good result I had previously got with Italian, I decided here again that I should also record my Chinese conversations as well. As soon as I said this to myself, I found a few Chinese speakers from my neighborhood who were available during the very next two weeks to help me adapt my conversations into Chinese and record them for me to take part in the conversations to re-listen and re-record, as needed, to practice.

After about three weeks of passionate and I would say intense learning, I felt ready to converse with people in real-life situations. It was then that I decided to go Flushing in Queens and Chinatown in Manhattan for some conversations.

This said, with Chinese being a complete new language for me, I felt somewhat a little bit wary about these upcoming trips to Chinatown. For this, I said to myself that I should look for some "conversation fillers" first, in case I would get stuck.

Some of you might ask by now what do I mean by conversation fillers? By conversation fillers, what I mean are short sentences such as "¿Que quieres decir? ("What do you mean?"), or "Qǐng zài shuō yí biàn!" ("Please say it again!"), or still "¿Puedes explicar un poco más lentamente lo que dices? ("Can you explain what you are saying a little bit more slowly?"). What these conversation fillers do is help you get your interlocutor to repeat or clarify what he or she is saying, while you try to digest what you have just heard or try to prepare to say the next sentence. The additional benefit of these fillers is that they not only helped the conversations become more interesting, but they also made them flow better. Just by saying "je ne sais pas si je suis d'accord avec toi" ("I don't know if I agree with you") or "stimmst du mir zu?" ("do you agree with me?"), they will make you look as if you are taking a position or asking for a position, while in fact helping you slow down your interlocutor.

While I did not need too much of these with Spanish or with Italian, but with Chinese being a completely different language, I told myself that I would need to have several conversation fillers handy before I would venture into Chinatown—and as it turned out, my fear was quite founded. In looking back, I don't know how many times I would have been forced to slow down or stop my conversations with people in Chinatown, if I had not thought of coming up with a list like the one below.

nǐ néng shuō dà sheng yīdiǎn ma?
("Can you speak louder?")

Zuìjìn hǎo ma?
("How have you been recently?")

Qǐngwèn nǐ shuō shénme?
("Please, what did you say?")

Qǐng nǐ zài shuō yī cì
("Please say it again")

One week later, I surprised my wife and children by speaking completely in Chinese with the Chinese Uber driver during the whole trip it took him to drive us from a Mongolian Hot Pot restaurant in Flushing back to our apartment in the Upper West Side.

Delighted by the confirmation that my method was also producing the same quick result with Chinese, I said to myself that it would be time to add some 10 more conversations to the previous 40 conversations. So, from 40 conversations they soon became 50 conversations. Below are the 10 new conversations I added to the list for your information.

Lesson 41: Buying books in some bookstore

Lesson 42: Attending a reception

Lesson 43: Visiting the manufacturing plant

Lesson 44: How much do you pay for your hotel bill?

Lesson 45: At the airport for the flight home

Lesson 46: Arriving at the gate

Lesson 47: Recovering from jet lag

Lesson 48: What to order at the restaurant?

Lesson 49: Doing some shopping at the mall

Lesson 50: Buying grocery for the work week

Chapter 15: How did I recover my Portuguese in two weeks for the Olympics Games in Rio?

Without being an athlete myself, I must say that I'm a fan of the Olympics Games—for both the friendship and the competitive spirit of the different sports events. This is the reason why, when I learned that the Olympics Games would be held in Rio in 2016, I said to myself that I should seize this opportunity to go to Brazil. I also saw this as an opportunity to recover my Portuguese, which I had somewhat lost, after I moved to Texas many years ago—with my wife and me so busy raising our three young kids.

With the above in mind, the good thing I had done was to have created a summary for Portuguese and stored it safely away in a green folder. The idea I had in mind was to eventually review it rather quickly to get the foundation going again. It is the content of the green folder that we will look at in this chapter.

Excited by the potential prospect of going to Brazil, I went ahead to look for the green folder. Thankfully I easily found the green folder, even though we had moved a few times. It was still new, as if I had just bought it yesterday. When I opened it, I was delighted to see about thirty pages, carefully stapled together, with a few pages of English and Portuguese cognates at the top, then several pages on verb tenses and, finally, several more pages on Portuguese parts of speech and syntax.

Rather than following the exact same thing I had done with French and Spanish, I was, this time around, interested in some new ways to ask questions in Portuguese by using interrogative words such as "que" ("what") or "quando" ("when").

Ex.

"Que você quer dezir?"
("What do you want to say?")
- - - - -
"Quando é o seu aniversário?"
("When is your birthday?")

After this, below is a summary of my notes on Portuguese personal subject pronouns, articles, nouns, and adjectives.

Personal subject pronouns:

A subject pronoun is what you will be using to show who carries out the action, event, or goes through a certain state of being, as we had previously referred to.

English Equivalent	Subject Pronoun Singular
I	Eu
You	Tu (mainly in Portugal)
You	Você (mainly in Brazil)
He	Ele
She	Ela

English Equivalent	Subject Pronoun Plural
We	Nós
You	Vós (mainly in Portugal)
You	Vocês (mainly in Brazil)
They	Eles/Elas

From the table above, you can see that there are many forms of "you" singular in Portuguese. Practically, Brazilians use "você" (with "vocês" being the plural), while people from Portugal will instead use "tu" (with "vós" being the plural). The key thing is to pay attention to the form people use where you are and adapt yourself to the situation.

Ex.
"Eu vejo"
("I see")

In the example above, "Eu" ("I") is the subject pronoun and "vejo" is the verb "ver" ("to see") in the first singular person of the present indicative tense. To this effect, I also wrote in a side note that, in Portuguese, the subject pronouns are practically never omitted, unlike Spanish.

Articles:

Like in English, there are two types of articles in Portuguese: indefinite and definite.

Indefinite Articles:

Whenever you want to refer to someone or something non-specific, that is when you use what is known in Portuguese as indefinite articles: "um", "uma", "uns," and "umas".

	Singular	Plural
Masculine	Um	Uns
Feminine	Uma	Umas

Ex.
"Uma árvore de fruta"
("A fruit tree ")
- - - -
"Uma mulher"
("A woman")

Definite articles:

When you want to refer to someone or something specific, you want to use definite articles as seen in the table below.

	Singular	Plural
Masculine	O	Os
Feminine	A	As

Ex.

"Sim, eu cozinho durante o fim de semana"

("Yes, I cook during the weekend")

That was it for pronouns, let's look at nouns now.

Nouns:

Unlike languages such as German or Russian, there is no noun of neutral gender in Portuguese. Most nouns in Portuguese end in "-a" for female gender such as "casa" ("house") or in "-o" for male gender masculine such as "tio" ("uncle"). Despite these general rules, exceptions exist when it comes to nouns that are derived from Greek, which are masculine even though they may end in "-a".

Ex.
"O mapa" ("The map"), "O dia" ("The day") or "O programa" ("The program"), etc.

This said, all nouns that end in "-dade", "-tude", "-ção" such as "cidade" ("city"), "universidade" ("university"), "virtude" ("virtue"), and "canção" ("song"), are all feminine.

At the same time, some nouns have the same form for both gender. Examples of these are: "pianista" ("pianist"), "cliente" ("client"), "dentista" ("dentist"), etc.

Like in French, Spanish and Italian, it is important, in speaking Portuguese, to know the gender of the noun because it will determine the form of article, the endings the adjective that describes it, etc.

To form the plural for nouns, below is the rule you should follow.

For a noun of masculine gender:

Normally, an "-s" will be added to the nouns' ending to form the plural of a masculine noun that ends in a vowel. If the masculine noun ends in a consonant, there are many different rules. For example, masculine nouns ending in "ul", "ol", "el" and "al", change the "-l" to "-is".

Ex.

"Uma sala"	"As salas"
("A room")	("The rooms")

"Um Animal"	"Os animais"
("An animal")	("The animals")

"O anzol"	"Os anzóis"
("The hook")	("the hooks")

For nouns of feminine gender.

Like the above, normally, an "-s" would be added to the nouns' ending to form the plural of a feminine noun that ends in a vowel. But if the feminine noun ends in a consonant, then you should add "-es" instead.

Ex.

"Uma loja"	"Umas lojas"
("A room")	("The rooms")

"Uma cidade"	"As cidades"
("A city")	("The cities")

Adjectives:

Adjectives are words we use to describe nouns. In Portuguese, adjectives must agree with the noun they describe in both gender and number. Normally, adjectives normally follow the nouns that they describe, some adjectives such as "bom" ("good"), "belo" ("nice"), and "grande" ("great", "big"), however, often precede the noun, as can be seen in the examples below.

Ex.
"Um grande homem"
("A great man")
- - - -
"Um homem grande"
("A big man")

Now, let's look at how we will form the plural for adjectives. In general, to make an adjective plural, add an "-s" to the end of the word "estrangeira" as in the example below.

Ex.
"Uma cozinha estrangeira"
("A foreign cuisine")

- - - -
"As cozinhas estrangeiras"
("The foreign cuisines")

English and Portuguese cognates:

Words which end in "-ly" and sometimes "-ely" in English usually end in "-mente" or "-amente" in Portuguese.

Ex.

| Finally | Finalmente |
| Completely | Completamente |

Words which end in "-ous" in English usually end in "-oso" in Portuguese.

Ex.

| Curious | Curioso |
| Precious | Precioso |

Words which end in "-al" in English usually end the same way in Portuguese.

Ex.

| Hospital | Hospital |
| Medical | Medical |

Words which end in "-ic" in English usually end in "-ico" in Portuguese.

Ex.

| Toxic | Tóxico |

| Critic | Crítico |

Words which end in "-id" in English usually end in "-ido" in Portuguese.

Ex.
| Rapid | Rápido |
| Liquid | Líquido |

Words that end in "-ary" in English will usually end in "-ario" in Portuguese.

Ex.
| Diary | Diário |
| Primary | Primário |

Words that end in "-ar" in English usually end in the same in Portuguese

Ex.
| Familiar | Familiar |
| Muscular | Muscular |

Words that end in "-ence" in English usually end in "-ência" in Portuguese.

Ex.
| Competence | Competência |
| Excellence | Excelência |

Words which end in "-ment" in English usually end in "-mento" in Portuguese.

Ex.

Aliment	Alimento
Document	Documento

All words that end in "-ty" in English usually end in "-dade" in Portuguese.

Ex.

City	Cidade
University	Universidade

Words that end in "-tion" in English usually end in "-ção" in Portuguese.

Ex.

Situation	Situação
Continuation	Continuação

Words which end in "-ent" in English usually end in "-ente" in Portuguese.

Ex.

Fluent	Fluent
Content	Contente

Portuguese verb tenses:

After cognates, my focus was on verbs, and below are the tenses I decided to focus on first.

1. Present tense:

The first thing to do in order to conjugate verbs in Portuguese is to know the conjugation group the verb belongs to. In Portuguese, there are three groups of conjugation which end in: "-ar", "-er," or "–ir".

The present tense of regular verbs of the first conjugation groups end in "-ar" such as in "cozinhar" ("to cook").

"cozinhar" - - - - - -> stem: "cozinh-"
   ("to cook")

	cozinh-ar
Eu (I)	cozinh-o
Tu (You)	cozinh-as
Você (You)	cozinh-a
Ele/Ela (He/She)	cozinh-a
Nós (We)	cozinh-amos
Vós (You)	cozinh-ais
Vocês (You)	cozinh-am
Eles/Elas (They/They)	cozinh-am

Ex.
"Você cozinha, certo?"
("You cook, right?")
- - - -
The present tense of regular verbs of the second conjugation groups end in "-er" such as in "viver" ("to live").

"viver" - - - - - -> stem: "viv-"

	viv-er
Eu (I)	viv-o
Tu (You)	viv-es
Você (You)	viv-e
Ele/Ela (He/She)	viv-e
Nós (We)	viv-emos
Vós (You)	viv-eis
Vocês (You)	viv-em
Eles/Elas (They/They)	viv-em

Ex.
"Meus pais vivem em Nova York"
("My parents live in New York")

The present tense of regular verbs of the second conjugation groups end in "-ir": such as in "compartir" ("to share").

"compartir" - - - - - -> stem: "compart-"

	compart-ir
Eu (I)	compart-o
Tu (You)	compart -es
Você (You)	compart -e
Ele/Ela (He/She)	compart -e

Nós (We)	compart -imos
Vós (You)	compart -is
Vocês (You)	compart -em
Eles/Elas (They/They)	compart -em

Despite my desire to avoid having to ever deal with all the rules and exceptions of irregular verbs (meaning verbs that do not follow any standard patterns in conjugations), there are some which I strongly felt the need to know by heart, in order to be able to converse as soon as possible.

Below are some of the irregular verbs which I chose to learn by heart.

1. "estar":
("to be")

	estar
Eu (I)	estou
Tu (You)	estás
Você (You)	está
Ele/Ela (He/She)	está
Nós (We)	estamos
Vós (You)	estais
Vocês (You)	estão
Eles/Elas (They/They)	estão

Ex.
"Estou em Nova Iorque"
("I'm in New York")

2. "ser":
("to be")

	ser
Eu (I)	sou
Tu (You)	és
Você (You)	é
Ele/Ela (He/She)	é
Nós (We)	somos
Vós (You)	sois
Vocês (You)	são
Eles/Elas (They/They)	são

Ex.
"Sou francês mas vivo na América"
("I'm French but I live in America")

- - - -
"ter"
("To have")

	ter
Eu (I)	tenho
Tu (You)	tens
Você (You)	tem
Ele/Ela (He/She)	tem

Nós (We)	temos
Vós (You)	tendes
Vocês (You)	têm
Eles/Elas (They/They)	têm

Ex.
"Eu tenho muitos amigos na universidade"
("I have many friends at the university")

- - - -

"fazer": ("to do"/"to make")

	fazer
Eu (I)	faço
Tu (You)	fazes
Você (You)	faz
Ele/Ela (He/She)	faz
Nós (We)	fazemos
Vós (You)	fazeis
Vocês (You)	fazem
Eles/Elas (They/They)	fazem

Ex.
"Fazem duas horas que estou esperando por meu amigo"
("I have been waiting on my friend for two hours")

2. Future tense:

Along with the present tense, below is what I wrote about the future tense. The good news here is that all of the endings for all of the conjugation groups are the same for the future tense: "-ei, -ás, -á, -emos, -eis, -āo," to be added to the infinitive, as can be seen below.

"-ar":
"comprar" ("to buy")

	compr-ar
Eu (I)	compr-arei
Tu (You)	compr-arás
Você (You)	compr-ará
Ele/Ela (He/She)	compr-ará
Nós (We)	compr-aremos
Vós (You)	compr-areis
Vocês (You)	compr-arāo
Eles/Elas (They/They)	compr-arāo

Ex.
"Eu comprarei um carro amanhā para ir à universidade"
("I will a buy a car tomorrow to go to the university")

- - - - - - - -
"-er":
"comer" ("to eat")

	com-er
Eu (I)	com-erei
Tu (You)	com-erás
Você (You)	com-erá

Ele/Ela (He/She)	com-erá
Nós (We)	com-eremos
Vós (You)	com-ereis
Vocês (You)	com-erão
Eles/Elas (They/They)	com-erão

Ex.
"Comeremos em um bom restaurante na próxima semana"
("We will eat at a good restaurant next week")

- - - -

"-ir":
"partir" ("to leave")

	part-ir
Eu (I)	part-irei
Tu (You)	part-irás
Você (You)	part-irá
Ele/Ela (He/She)	part-irá
Nós (We)	part-iremos
Vós (You)	part-ireis
Vocês (You)	part-irão
Eles/Elas (They/They)	part-irão

Ex.
"Viverei na Espanha com muito prazer"
("I will live with pleasure in Spain")

3. Preterit tense:

If you have interacted with Brazilians, you realize how often they like to use the preterit tense for practically anything related to the past—unless dictated very specifically by some kind of special circumstances. This is why I decided to learn the preterit tense first rather than the imperfect tense.

To conjugate regular "-ar" verbs in the preterit tense, simply drop the infinitive ending ("-ar") and add one of the following:

Eu (I)	-ei
Tu (You)	-aste
Você (You)	-ou
Ele/Ela (He/She)	-amos
Nós (We)	-astes
Vós (You)	-aram
Vocês (You)	-aram
Eles/Elas (They/They)	-aram

Applying the above rule, the following is the result you will get for:

"-ar":
"comprar" ("to buy")

	compr-ar
Eu (I)	compr-ei
Tu (You)	compr-aste
Você (You)	compr-ou
Ele/Ela (He/She)	compr-ou
Nós (We)	compr-amos
Vós (You)	compr-astes
Vocês (You)	compraram
Eles/Elas (They/They)	compr-aram

Ex.
"Eu comprei um carro ontem"
("I bought a car yesterday")

To conjugate regular "-er" verbs in the preterit indicative tense, simply drop the ending ("-er") and add one of the following endings instead:

| Eu (I) | -i |

Tu (You)	-este
Você (You)	-eu
Ele/Ela (He/She)	-eu
Nós (We)	-emos
Vós (You)	-estes
Vocês (You)	-eram
Eles/Elas (They/They)	-eram

Applying the above rule, the following is the result you will get for "comer" ("to eat"):

	com-er
Eu (I)	com-i
Tu (You)	com-este
Você (You)	com-eu
Ele/Ela (He/She)	com-eu
Nós (We)	com-emos
Vós (You)	com-estes
Vocês (You)	com-eram
Eles/Elas (They/They)	com-eram

Ex.

"Eu comi com minha amiga ontem"
("I ate with my friend yesterday")

To conjugate regular "-ir" verbs in the preterit tense, simply drop the ending ("-ir") and add one of the following endings instead:

Eu (I)	-i
Tu (You)	-iste
Você (You)	-iu
Ele/Ela (He/She)	-iu
Nós (We)	-imos
Vós (You)	-istes
Vocês (You)	-iram
Eles/Elas (They/They)	-iram

Applying the above rule, the following is the result you will get for "competir" ("to compete"):

	compet-ir
Eu (I)	compet-i
Tu (You)	compet-iste

Você (You)	compet-iu
Ele/Ela (He/She)	compet-iu
Nós (We)	compet-imos
Vós (You)	compet-istes
Vocês (You)	compet-iram
Eles/Elas (They/They)	compet-iram

Ex.
"Meu irmão competiu uma vez nos Jogos Olímpicos"
("My brother competed once in the Olympics")

Here we are at the end of my notes on Portuguese verb tenses, which I thought I would need for Rio.

Following what I had successfully done with both Italian and Chinese, I decided to look for some people who would speak Portuguese to do some quick translation with me and record my conversations for me—and fast.

After two weeks or so of daily intensive practice, I started to feel that I could speak and understand Portuguese again.

For illustrative purposes, below are some of the Portuguese conversations, along with examples of conversation fillers in Portuguese, out of a total of 40 conversations which I used for my Portuguese recovery.

Conversations:

Lesson 23: Have you ever tried yoga?

[student 1] Você já ouviu falar de yoga?
[student 2] Sim, mas eu nunca aprendi. Você aprendeu isso?
[student 1] Sim, eu aprendi. De fato, eu vou ter a minha aula de ioga esta manhã.
[student 2] Fantástico! Há um monte de pessoas na classe?
[student 1] Sim, há cerca de quinze pessoas.
[student 2] Eu vejo. É realmente relaxante?
[student 1] Sim, é realmente relaxante. Eu gosto muito. Você quer tentar?
[student 2] Sim, eu vou gostar.

[student 1] Have you ever heard of yoga?
[student 2] Yes, but I have not ever learned it. Have you learned it?
[student 1] Yes, I have. And as a matter of fact, I am going to have my yoga lesson this morning.
[student 2] Fantastic! Are there a lot of people in the class?
[student 1] Yes, there are. Around fifteen people.
[student 2] I see. Is it really relaxing?
[student 1] Yes, it is really relaxing. I love it a lot. Do you want to try it?
[student 2] Yes, I will like to.

- - - - -

Lesson 24: Is there a post office nearby?
[student 1] Você sabe se há uma agência de correios perto daqui?
[student 2] Por que?
[student 1] Eu tenho um envelope e um pacote para enviar.
[student 2] Sim, há uma agência de correios a cinco minutos a pé.
[student 1] Isso é ótimo. Eu estarei de volta em dez

minutos.
[student 2] Não tem problema. Eu vou te esperar.
[student 1] Obrigado. Eu não vou demorar.
[student 2] Não se preocupe comigo.

[student 1] Do you know if there is a post office near here?
[student 2] Why?
[student 1] I have an envelope and a package to send.
[student 2] Yes, there is a post office five minutes away on foot.
[student 1] That is great. I will be back in ten minutes.
[student 2] No problem. I will wait for you.
[student 1] Thank you. I will not be long.
[student 2] Do not worry about me.

Conversation fillers:

O que você quer dizer?
("What do you mean?")

Você pode repetir o que você disse?
("Can you repeat what you just said?")

Pode explicar o que você acabou de dizer?
("Can you explain what you just said?")

Você pode falar mais devagar?
("Can you speak more slowly?")

Você pode falar um pouco mais alto?
("Can you speak a little bit louder?")

Besides a slightly different way of pronouncing some words, which could somewhat scare some people away, I find Portuguese to be a rather easy and fun language to learn, especially if you already know Spanish and Italian.

In the end, due to the dire situation with some health hazards in Brazil at the time, I did not to go Rio. This said, I'm glad that the buildup of such a great expectation had led me to successfully recover my Portuguese so quickly—in about two weeks.

While it has become somewhat common to hear people speak Spanish in public in New York, it is not the case with Portuguese. This is the reason why it makes me smile when I hear some of my Brazilian neighbors in New York speak in Portuguese while in the elevator with me. Whenever I turned around to address them in Portuguese: "Vocês moram aqui?" ("Do you live here?"). One of them would readily respond to the question: "Sim" ("Yes") or "Não, somos turistas. Somos aqui para visitar amigos" ("No, we are tourists. We are here to visit friends"). At that time, one of them would normally take over and ask me: "Você mora aqui?" ("Do you live here?"), to which I would respond: "Sim" ("Yes"). Just as I would finish my sentence, one of them would pursue with something like: "O seu português é muito bom" ("Your Portuguese is very good"), to which I would invariably say: "Abrigodo" ("Thank you"). Then either one of them would say: "É incrível ver alguém falando português como você" ("It is amazing to see someone speaking Portuguese as well as you do"). Usually, it was at this very moment that the elevator bell would make a small noise, signaling to us that either they had arrived at their floor or I had arrived at mine. It was then that we would say almost all at the same time: "Até a próxima vez!" ("See you next time!") with a smile and some light happiness in the air from a rather short—but quite unexpected—encounter between a young Brazilian couple and an Asian-looking guy in Portuguese right in the middle of Manhattan.

Encouraged once again by the speed at which I was able to recover Portuguese, I went ahead to add another 10 more conversations to the previous 50 conversations. So, from 50 conversations, they soon became 60 conversations. Below are the 10 new conversations I added to the list.

Lesson 51: Buying books in some

Lesson 50: Buying grocery for the work week

Lesson 51: Picking up some relatives at the airport

Lesson 52: Driving family relatives around town

Lesson 53: Dropping the relatives back at the airport

Lesson 54: Waiting at home for a new cable TV installation

Lesson 55: Watching a foreign film on the new cable TV

Lesson 56: Accepting a delivery at home

Lesson 57: Exercising at the gym

Lesson 58: Going back to work

Lesson 59: Taking a break at the office

Lesson 60: Reading the newspaper in a bistro

With 60 conversations and a lot of grammar and verbs stuffs, things started to get big. To make everything clearer, I divided the 60 conversations and the grammar and verb summaries around three layers of increasing knowledge, each with 20 conversations and a corresponding portion of grammar and verbs summary.

The way I structured these three layers, it is as if they were three levels of maturity (with people being able to speak the new target language from level 1):

Maturity Level 1 (Beginner): for learners who just
started but who would be knowledgeable enough after the first month to be able to have decent conversations with people in the new language about daily life topics, using simple vocabulary and three or four simple verb tenses. (Think of the level of elementary and middle school students, with a given language from a given country.)

Maturity Level 2 (Intermediate): for learners who have previously achieved some ease in speaking with people in the new target language as a beginner, but he or she, this time around, will have a more elaborate vocabulary and know some more sophisticated verb tenses. (Think of the high school students, with a given language from a given country.)

Maturity Level 3 (Advanced): for learners who are on their way to speaking with even more proficiency, capable of explaining everything they want to say—using a more elaborate vocabulary and most of the verb tenses. (Think of the college or university students, with a given language from a given country.)

Maturity – Level 1 (Beginner):

L1.1: The conversations:

Lesson 1: Exchanging greetings between friends

Lesson 2: Inquiring about a friend's birthday

Lesson 3: Telling a friend about your family

Lesson 4: Talking about one another family's house

Lesson 5: Cooking or ordering in?

Lesson 6: Asking about the outside of the house

Lesson 7: Talking about sports

Lesson 8: Cooking at home or eating out

Lesson 9: Talking about going to the movie

Lesson 10: Talking about one another's work schedule

Lesson 11: Going to the shopping mall

Lesson 12: Do you have some other friends in town

Lesson 13: What about going on vacation together

Lesson 14: How should we go on vacation together

Lesson 15: Inquiring about the weather at the beach

Lesson 16: How about having lunch together?

Lesson 17: How about dropping by the chocolate shop?

Lesson 18: How about going to the flowers market now?

Lesson 19: How about going to the fair?

Lesson 20: Why not have a picnic in the countryside museums on spare time during the trip

- - - -

L1.2: Essence of Grammar and Verbs

Introduction

Types of sentences

Positive sentences

Active sentences
    Interrogative sentences
    Passive sentences
    Commanding sentences

Negative sentences

Review of the different parts of speech
Nouns

Pronouns
    Personal subject pronouns
    Direct object pronouns
    Indirect object pronouns

Articles
    Indefinite articles
    Definite articles

Adjectives
    Variable adjectives

Adverbs
    Adverbs of quantity
    Adverbs of manner

Prepositions

Conjunctions
    Coordinating conjunctions

Interjections

Verbs

> Impersonal verbs/expressions
> Present indicative tense
> Future indicative tense
> Past indicative tenses
> Present perfect indicative tense
> Imperfect indicative tense
> Preterit indicative tense

Numerical

Cardinal numbers

How to build up fast your vocabulary.

- - - -

Maturity – Level 2 (Intermediate):

L 2.1: The conversations:

Lesson 21: Why not stop for lunch on the road?

Lesson 22: Do you know how to play piano?

Lesson 23: Have you ever tried yoga?

Lesson 24: Is there a post office nearby?

Lesson 25: I'm having an appointment with my doctor

Lesson 26: How about going to the zoo?

Lesson 27: Admiring animals at the zoo

Lesson 28: How about going to a concert?

Lesson 29: How about going for a walk in the park?

Lesson 30: What about having dinner together?

Lesson 31: How about dropping by a bookstore?

Lesson 32: Talking about an upcoming birthday

Lesson 33: How was the meal?

Lesson 34: Booking a trip online

Lesson 35: Preparing the baggage

Lesson 36: Are you at the airport yet?

Lesson 37: Have you landed yet?

Lesson 38: Arriving at the hotel

Lesson 39: What time to wake up tomorrow morning?

Lesson 40: Visiting museums on spare during the trip

- - - -

L 2.2: Essence of Grammar and Verbs

Pronouns (cont'd)
Reflexive personal pronouns
Interrogative pronouns

Adjectives (cont'd)
Invariable adjectives
Possessive adjectives
Interrogative adjectives
Demonstrative adjectives

Adverbs (cont'd)
Adverbs of affirmation
Adverbs of negation
Adverbs of place
Adverbs of time

Prepositions (cont'd)

Comparisons (between adjectives and between adverbs)

More on verbs (cont'd)
Impersonal verbs/expressions (cont'd)
Near future indicative tense
Immediate past indicative tense
Reflexive present indicative tense
Present imperative indicative tense
Future perfect indicative tense
Past perfect indicative tense
Present conditional tense

Present subjunctive tense

Numerical (cont'd)

Cardinal numbers

Ordinal numbers

Days

How to build up fast your vocabulary (cont'd).

- - - -

Maturity – Level 3 (Advanced):

L 3.1: The conversations:

Lesson 41: Buying books in some bookstore

Lesson 42: Attending a reception

Lesson 43: Visiting the manufacturing plant

Lesson 44: How much do you pay for your hotel bill?

Lesson 45: At the airport for the flight home

Lesson 46: Arriving at the gate

Lesson 47: Recovering from jet lag

Lesson 48: What to order at the restaurant?

Lesson 49: Doing some shopping at the mall

Lesson 50: Buying grocery for the work week

Lesson 51: Picking up some relatives at the airport

Lesson 52: Driving family relatives around town

Lesson 53: Dropping the relatives back at the airport

Lesson 54: Waiting at home for a new cable TV installation

Lesson 55: Watching a foreign film on the new cable TV

Lesson 56: Accepting a delivery at home

Lesson 57: Exercising at the gym

Lesson 58: Going back to work

Lesson 59: Taking a break at the office

Lesson 60: Reading the newspaper in a bistro

- - - -

L 3. 2: Essence of Grammar and Verbs

Pronouns (cont'd)

Prepositional pronouns
Relative pronouns
Indefinite pronouns
Demonstrative pronouns
Possessive pronouns

Adjectives (cont'd)
Indefinite adjectives

Adverbs (cont'd)
Adverbs of frequency (time)
Adverbs of direction

Conjunctions (cont'd)
Subordinating conjunctions

More on verbs (cont'd)
Impersonal verbs/expressions (cont'd)
Gerunds
Progressive tenses
Present infinitive
Past infinitive
Imperfect subjunctive tense
Past conditional tense

Numerical (cont'd)
Cardinal numbers
Ordinal numbers

Months

Seasons

Telling times

Telling dates

Fractions and percentages

Collective numbers

Fractions

Decimal numbers

How to build up fast your vocabulary (cont'd).

Chapter 16: All the things you should not do in learning to speak a foreign language in a nutshell

Given all the details we have gone through together until now, I think the time has arrived for me to sum up what I think you should not do while learning a new language.

Do not learn to speak, read, and write at the same time. My recommendation is to focus on speaking first.

Do not let things drag out too long. If you do not limit your learning timeline to a short timeframe, you might end up being forced to cease your learning and completely stop your studies, sooner or later, due to other life responsibilities.

Do not let yourself be overwhelmed by too much material early on or all at once. Learn the basics first and then move towards more intermediate and advanced topics, depending on your need. To this effect, do not hesitate to refer to my three-level summary template as inspiration.

Do not hesitate to practice speaking before you think you know all the grammatical rules. Try to find an opportunity to speak from day one; and when there is no one to speak with, speak with yourself, as I did many years ago. Also, remember that you should not feel bad translating what you want to say from your base language into the target language—at least, during the first weeks. While I do not recommend that you translate anything from your base language while speaking with people in the target language, I still believe that you should not feel guilty as if you had committed a mortal sin if you happen to catch yourself translating—at least at the beginning. As you know, Rome was not built in a day, so give yourself some slack in building up your knowledge of the new language first before you can speak without translating.

Do not fear grammar or verbs. While they have been presented traditionally as a set of rather dry rules and exceptions to remember by heart, I always look at grammar and verbs as a helping hand, helping me learn to build new sentences and knowledge on my own—to give me more freedom. This said, I would recommend that you do not spend too much time on the rules of irregular verbs but, instead, only "google" them if you need.

Don't forget to leverage the conversation fillers to the maximum. Try to identify some conversation fillers to help you keep the conversations flowing.

Do not skip any days. The reason why I suggest this is because I have seen the huge difference between learning once or twice a week and five consecutive days a week. So, if you can, learn every day, even if for only 20 or 40 minutes a day, let's say, for thirty consecutive days.

Do not do anything once you have started your language lesson. Unlike what we have heard, don't expect to speak French, German, Russian, or Chinese naturally and in no time by only listening to some recordings while running on the treadmill or while driving to work. Having successfully learnt many languages all these years, I know that this has never worked and will never work.

Don't forget to practice speaking with people outside of the lessons. Not only should you start speaking from day one during your first lesson but also try to practice speaking outside of your lessons, and as often as you can. Remember, nothing can replace practice, and the more you practice speaking and conversing with people, the more you will become comfortable at speaking and conversing with people in the new language.

While the above is what you should not do in learning a new language, in the next chapter, I am going to talk with you about what you should do to avoid losing a language you have learned.

Chapter 17: How not to forget a foreign language you have learned?

While this may sound obvious, the only way not to forget a foreign language is to use it regularly in your daily life. Without practice, there is no reason why you would not to lose one of your languages. This could happen to anybody, as it had happened to me.

For a healthy maintenance, I expect that it would take you between ten or fifteen minutes a day or, at least, every other day to maintain a working knowledge of a foreign language. Whether you spend time watching TV, listening to the radio, reading the newspaper or speaking with someone, anything would help more than nothing, knowing that I believe that speaking will be what you
need to practice the most. But the key thing is that you should spend ten or fifteen minutes a day, if not, every other day, to maintain a good working foreign language.

Besides reading or watching TV or listening to the radio, what if you do not find anyone to speak with? In my opinion, that should not be a problem as I had gotten used to speaking with myself many years ago. To remedy this situation, find some samples of conversations and, as needed, practice speaking with yourself if there is no one around to practice with you. The best would be to find a software with conversations for you to listen to and to record yourself taking part in these conversations to re-listen. But, do not fall into the trap of focusing more on the "perfect" pronunciation rather than on your understanding of your part of the conversations and of the conversations as the whole. In many countries of the world, people can understand you even if your pronunciation is not perfect. So, instead of focusing only on the pronunciation (especially when it is done away from the threads of the overall conversations), you should also focus on the conversational side, with you talking to record to re-listen and, eventually, to compare with the native speaker's recordings. As you continue to practice, not only will your speaking skills improve, your pronunciation will also improve before too long.

Now what if you do not have time nor all the opportunity needed to do the above to maintain a good working knowledge of your foreign language or languages? Below is my recommendation as to what to do. Rather than focusing only on what to do after you lose the command of one of your languages, my recommendation will deal with both what you should do before (while you are actively learning) and what you should do after (you have lost the command of one of your languages).

Before it happens:

The first thing to do is to make sure that you have reached a good level of proficiency in that foreign language while you are still actively learning it. What this means is that you should learn and find as many opportunities as possible to speak and take part in conversations in that foreign language, even after you got the feeling that you have had a good grasp of it. Learn some more, listen and speak some more, like I did. Learn, listen and speak until you feel like the new language comes naturally to you without you having to stumble looking for words.

Another critical thing you would need to do is to spend some time creating some sort of grammatical summaries—either by writing something completely new to your taste or by inspiring from the examples or templates I have shared with you in the book. Disposing of grammatical summary will help ensure that you can recover the grammatical and verbs side of that foreign language fast, if you need to. This is like, as you would remember, what I did with Portuguese when I was trying to recover it.

After it happens:

Now, what should you do if you still happen to have lost the command of one of your foreign languages? Well, this is when you will need to go to that language summary I just suggested above that you create. From two things, one: either you have created a summary or you have not. If you have, then you may be lucky in that you may be well positioned to recover the theoretical side of that foreign language fast, while losing no time with preparation work. But, if you happen to have not created any summary, then you should either find a concise grammar or a few books to go through to create your own summary now or else a software with such a summary—along with some conversations to listen to and to take part in, to record yourself speaking to re-listen and, eventually, to compare with the native speakers' own recordings of the very conversations.

While it is a pain to lose or to have lost the command of one of your languages, you now know, at least, what you should do before it happens (either to prevent or to help speed up the recovery effort) or after it happens.

Chapter 18: Epilogue

Here we are at the end of this book on my journey—up to now—through the wonderland of language learning. I hope that you have enjoyed reading the book as much as I have writing it. To make this book as complete and as tangible as possible, I have told you everything significant I remember that I did, how I did it, and how the way I learned was, at first, rather random before I was able to evolve it into something that makes it possible to learn a new language better and at a faster pace.

Given all the details I have shared with you throughout the book, some of you may think that I'm a highly skilled linguist or someone exceptionally good at languages. The reality is far from that. Far from trying to know all about the origins of human languages and far from being a genius, all I have wanted is to discover a new perspective, to make friends as well as to have fun and to know more about other people's cultures and cooking—to know why and how they think, speak, cook, and eat differently from us.

Even though I have been successful at learning many foreign languages from different families of languages throughout the years, I know that I'm not an exception. This is the reason why I know that you should be able to achieve the same result if you diligently follow my approach and method. If you do, you will be surprised to see that you will be on your way to speaking a new language soon—in 1 month.

Made in the USA
Columbia, SC
13 November 2017